3991
ED

School, Family and
Community Interaction

Published in cooperation with
the Milken Institute
for Job & Capital Formation

The Milken Institute
Series in Economics and Education

Series Editor
Lewis C. Solmon

Making Schools Work: A View from the Firing Lines, edited by Cheryl L. Fagnano and Katherine Nouri Hughes

School, Family and Community Interaction: A View from the Firing Lines, edited by Cheryl L. Fagnano and Beverly Z. Werber

School, Family and Community Interaction

A View from the Firing Lines

EDITED BY
Cheryl L. Fagnano and
Beverly Z. Werber

Milken Family Foundation

Westview Press
BOULDER • SAN FRANCISCO • OXFORD

The Milken Institute Series in Economics and Education

Copyright © 1994 by the Milken Institute for Job & Capital Formation

Published in 1994 in the United States of America by Westview Press, Inc., 5500 Central Avenue, Boulder, Colorado 80301-2877, and in the United Kingdom by Westview Press, 36 Lonsdale Road, Summertown, Oxford OX2 7EW

A CIP catalog record for this book is available from the Library of Congress.
ISBN 0-8133-2335-5

Printed and bound in the United States of America

The paper used in this publication meets the requirements
∞ of the American National Standard for Permanence of Paper
for Printed Library Materials Z39.48-1984.

10   9   8   7   6   5   4   3   2   1

Contents

Foreword

The essays in this volume are based on remarks and papers given at the annual Milken Family Foundation National Education Conference held in Los Angeles in March 1993.

The gathering is the professional development component of the Foundation's National Educator Awards program. Conceived by Lowell and Michael Milken in the early 1980s, the program was formally established in California in 1987 and offers substantial individual awards to professionals in elementary and secondary schools around the country. Its chief aims are to recognize and reward educators—150 in 1993—who have made and continue to make significant contributions to the education of children; to heighten public appreciation of the teaching profession thereby encouraging talented men and women to enter the field of education; and to contribute to the professional development of recipients by bringing them together with distinguished representatives of the profession and a range of public officials for a three-day conference exploring compelling education issues. The program honors educators in participating states, which, in 1993, numbered 25.

Lewis C. Solmon, President
Milken Institute for Job & Capital Formation

Acknowledgments

The editors gratefully acknowledge the valuable assistance of several people in the production of this book. David Weinrot of the Milken Institute provided extensive research support. Lawrence Lesser, of the Milken Family Foundations, contributed the technical expertise required to produce this volume. Laura Janssen's mastery of desktop publishing as well as her bountiful patience ensured a polished copy. And we wish to thank all the National Educator Award Recipients and Conference speakers whose ideas and innovative practices made this book possible.

Cheryl L. Fagnano
Beverly Z. Werber

PART ONE

Introduction

1

Families, Communities and Schools: A Perspective from the Foundations

Lowell Milken

The convergence of care-giving responsibilities in schools and on educators—however challenging—is an enormous opportunity for all of us concerned with bringing order out of the chaos that prevails in so much of our contemporary life. The Foundations of the Milken Families chose "The Interaction of Families, Communities and Schools" as the topic for the 1993 National Education Conference in order to seize that opportunity as well as to draw on the considerable experience we have gained from working on all three fronts.

The Milken Family Foundation National Education Conferences are an occasion for all of us—community activists, public officials and some of the most creative and talented educators in the country—to pool our experience; for solutions to the most intractable social problems can be found when determined and imaginative people work together.

The Foundations of the Milken Families are the life-long commitment my brother Michael and I have had to helping build a strong and secure society. As college students in the late 1960s, it became clear to both of us that to achieve that goal meant helping connect people with opportunities for improving their own lives. It meant creating programs that would enfranchise people and entrust them with responsibility.

Our early activities working with educators and community members gained considerable momentum when we formally established the Foundations in 1982 with the mission to help people help themselves and those around them to lead productive and satisfying lives.

Editor's Note: The following is adapted from the opening presentation of the 1993 National Education Conference.

"Helping people help themselves" speaks to the building of human resources, of human capital. Helping people "help those around them" addresses the strengthening of what University of Chicago sociologist James Coleman has termed social capital, the productive capacity inherent in the relations between and among people (1990). Finally, helping people "to lead productive and satisfying lives" aims to release and deploy these forms of capital through meaningful job opportunities that allow people to lead lives of creativity and purpose.

We have pursued this mission in the areas of education, community services, health care and medical research and human welfare—each a field that lends itself to the development of the individual and that recognizes people's essential needs. We have also believed from the start that these are areas in which our resources of ideas, time and funding would have the greatest effect. The 11 years since our founding have borne out that belief.

We are especially pleased to see how our mission is advanced by the programs we have created. In each funding area we have conceived programs that are significant investments in human development, that are increasing the store of social capital, that tackle problems at the source, and that provide some astonishing evidence of what can be done when people are helped to help themselves.

We drew deep upon our endowment of experience in working directly with schools, communities and families as we explored the topic of the 1993 Conference. And that topic is urgent. For what was once a continuum of care—from family, to school, to community—has been densely compressed. Although the responsibilities of many primary institutions have been rerouted into schools, often jamming the circuits of effective education, schools are not the only institutions to suffer from this collapsing of responsibilities. Today, community centers provide mental and physical health services, places of worship feed and shelter the homeless, and libraries do duty for day care centers.

Our most basic care-giving institutions have been elaborately undermined over the last generation, and the impact affects all social and economic strata. Poverty in America takes many forms, and though most are rooted in economic disadvantage, other kinds of poverty—of purpose and will—are eroding our social and moral base. It is the root system, then, that must be restored to health, and until it is, we are merely making surface adjustments to whatever problem we may try to treat.

As the Foundations evaluate the programs we create and work with, we continue to ask: What are the underpinnings of these troubled circumstances? Let's look first at the family.

Family

A recent report published by the multi-disciplinary Council on Families in America noted, "The evidence is strong and growing that the current generation of children and youth is the first in our nation's history to be less well off—psychologically, socially, economically and morally—than their parents were at the same age" (Council on Families in America, 1993). This shift is ominously reflected in the struggle of today's families.

While pessimists argue the family is self-destructing, optimists hold that it is just diversifying. Whatever the glow or shadow through which one views the American family, in little more than a generation there has been a radical change in the norm.

As recently as 1960, 70 percent of U.S. families included two parents—married and living together—with a working father and a mother who stayed home to mind the children. Today, fewer than 7 percent of all families in the United States fit that description (Martin, 1992). The "diversification" of today's family effectively precludes an "average," for in addition to the small minority resembling yesterday's norm, today's families include two-parent families in which both parents leave home to work; single-parent families—of which 90 percent are headed by women; two-parent families comprised of step-relations, half-relations, adopted relations and same sex couples; and an increasing number of adults, both married and single, who do not have children and have moved back with their parents. Today, quite simply, there is no typical family (Hamburg, 1992).[1]

Though a host of forces has conspired to subvert the family, its anemic condition stems from two basic deficits—of resources and time—the resource deficit primarily affecting the disadvantaged and the time deficit affecting both disadvantaged and mainstream families (Hewlett, 1991).[2]

The resource deficit is about poverty and what comes with it. It is about the 20 percent of all U.S. children, the 38 percent of Latino children and the 45 percent of black children who are living in poverty (Outtz, 1993).[3] It is about the 37 million Americans who have no health insurance whatever (Hamburg, 1992). It is the degradation of people who cannot find work or who cannot make ends meet on what they do earn. It is the despair of the adult who cannot read and of the child who goes to school hungry. It is the calamity—for all of us—of the person of any age who does not have a bed to call his own.

The time deficit is about short-changing children of the very thing they need most—the attention of those who care for them—a circle that should, and used to, radiate far beyond two parents and include not only grandparents and relatives but also friends and neighbors.

But today it is a very different story. The resource deficit has made a large and negative contribution to the time deficit. Today, in many cases out of sheer economic necessity, two-thirds of all mothers are in the paid work force (Outtz, 1993). For many, the professional work week has topped 50 hours (Hewlitt, 1991). By the age of 16, nearly half of all youngsters whose parents are married will see those marriages end in divorce (Hamburg, 1992). And one-quarter of all children are born to single mothers (Outtz, 1993). The toll of these pressures is etched deep on a generation of children who, quite literally, do not know what to expect of life.

Whether parents intend to leave their children on their own or not, the time deficit means at least one sure thing for the youngster on the receiving end: a feeling of loneliness and neglect. And when children are put on their own before they are ready, they compensate for the loss—often in ways that are dangerous and destructive.

Painfully revealing of the ground that has been lost by and in the family is the fact that the importance of parental involvement in children's lives and education needs to be explained. But it does, and it needs far-reaching reinforcement, which we are working to provide through programs that not only engage parents in their children's education but that connect mothers and fathers with their role as parents.

It is the rare family, then, who is untouched by some sort of want or fear or isolation, and taken together, these conditions have created an emergency for anyone trying to raise a child to be responsible, self-assured and thoughtful to others.

Community

There was a time—a time I remember well—when the community helped connect people. Growing up, I lived exactly six blocks from the Hesby Street Elementary School in L.A.'s San Fernando Valley, and anonymous I was not. Most of the people on those six blocks knew me, knew my family, and God forbid that I might stretch the limits of acceptable behavior in any direction. The people around me helped define the frontier between right and wrong. We knew what was expected of us, and we knew that people cared about us.

Back then, the community not only supplied much of the mortar holding families together and joining them with neighbors, it linked people with their work and what they did with their free time. It was the community that held together our essential and abiding institutions, and it joined their authority figures, too. Mothers and fathers, teachers and principals, the minister, the rabbi, the coach and family doctor were in touch with each other. Children knew this, and they thrived on it.

Today's communities lack the magnetic force once supplied by the stable family, by other care-giving institutions, particularly religious, and by the values they generated. What remains in all too many communities is the frightening environment defined primarily by what it lacks—by the absence of trust, the absence of respect and the absence of security—and in this vacuum roils the violence that makes such negative investments as metal detectors necessary in schools, that has Americans spending five billion dollars a year on home security systems, and that explains why, in Los Angeles, you have a greater chance of dying from a bullet wound than in a traffic accident. It is hardly surprising that the citizens of Los Angeles rank crime, gangs and violence as the number one priority for elected officials to address (Clifford, 1993).

Although the conditions that produce a daily fear for one's safety must not be tolerated, unfortunately, all too often they are. The social organism, like the human organism, has a great capacity for adapting, often at its own expense. Our lexicon of fear, for example, already includes a term— "drive-by shooting"—to describe the neighborhood terrorism that reigns in Los Angeles and other cities across the country. Such terms ratify violence and encourage us to adapt to what we should abhor.

And the Greater Los Angeles community is a unique case in point. Covering an area of more than 4,000 square miles, with a population of nearly 9 million and with residents who speak close to 100 different languages, socially and geographically the imperatives of Los Angeles demand a new understanding of community and of neighbors. What happened in Los Angeles in the spring of 1992 spelled out a clear message for all concerned with the restoration of civic health and dignity to our almost impossibly strained urban communities all across the country.

First, all people, but especially those living in conditions of poverty and despair, must be given greater possibilities for helping themselves. Once they have, they must accept the responsibility attached to those possibilities. This is a matter of taking responsibility not only for oneself but also for the community in which one lives.

Second, we must work to increase our store of both human and social capital. We need to understand that investments in all forms of capital— physical, financial, human and social—complement one another, and when we revitalize the community, we foster the environment in which our investments in education and jobs will flourish (Putnam, 1993).[4]

And third, theoretical solutions proffered from a distance do not work. No solution will ever get to the root of any problem unless it is carried out by people working with one another in the community.

Schools

On the basis of our work with hundreds of community organizations, we believe that the trends and accommodations that are destabilizing communities across the country *can* be reversed.

I have an example in mind—a school that has become a social invention in the hands of an unusually talented and tenacious principal. The school is Vaughn Street Elementary, and the principal is Yvonne Chan, a 1991 Milken Family Foundation National Educator Award Recipient from the Pacoima section of the San Fernando Valley of Los Angeles.

Dr. Chan was called into Vaughn Street three years ago to replace an incumbent who had to be removed from the school site due to repeated threats on her life by local gangs. What Dr. Chan inherited was the school equivalent of the community vacuum—an essential institution that was actually generating mistrust and ill-will. With those in positions of authority only lamenting the external factors that had been thrust upon the school and its educators, student achievement was abysmal. Not only was no one willing to take responsibility for it, those in the positions of responsibility—teachers and parents—were blaming each other.

Yvonne Chan says she is neither a principal nor a negotiator. She calls herself a relationship-builder, and she sees the heart of her job as getting people to work together, which she does. But as every educator knows, relationships are not built solely out of good intentions. People need to see what they are working on and working toward. They need projects that are attainable, such as the construction and staffing by parents of the Vaughn Family Center—a model of comprehensive and preventive social service delivery—providing everything from health check-ups, family counseling, and child care to drug abuse prevention, employment referrals and emergency aid.

In less than three years, not only has Vaughn Street regained a secure academic footing nurturing even the very youngest children throughout its "school-readiness network"; not only has it become a safe haven for gang members willing to play by a responsible adult's rules; today, it is the magnetic center of a community where educators, parents and community caregivers of all kinds reinforce each others' strengths.

Although the imagination and energy that went into turning around Vaughn Street are common denominators among the educators gathered annually for the National Education Conference, they certainly do not describe the norm. On the contrary: Schools in every setting across the country find themselves unequal to the demands and responsibilities shifted to them by broken families and nonfunctioning communities, and their primary task of teaching is radically undermined.

Consider the ramifications of this cross-section of data:

Only 71 percent of American students graduate from high school, versus 94 percent in Japan and 91 percent in Germany (Orgel, 1992), and the 700,000 students who drop out of school each year (Hamburg, 1992), cost our nation nearly $300 billion in lost lifetime earnings and foregone taxes (Orgel, 1992).

In the United States today, 20 percent—that is 36 million people—are functionally illiterate, which means they cannot read or write at the eighth-grade level (Hewlitt, 1991).

Only 3 percent of high school seniors can read at the level that will be required by 90 percent of the jobs created over the next 15 years (Orgel, 1992).

These are not numbers to be absorbed. They are lives to be saved and losses to be prevented.

On the basis of what we continue to hear from the hundreds of educators we work with, it is a challenge that can be met. We know that the circumstances of educators vary enormously according to geography, demography and socioeconomic condition. But we also know that educators and their schools can adapt, and that attitudes and practices that may be considered foreign to American educators can, in many cases, be transplanted in our schools with great success.

The Foundations' Evolving Mission

The family, the community and the school have become fragile entities in the last generation, and a principal reason is the lack of security that has come to define modern life. Restoring the security of the family, the community and the nation is a complex endeavor. In the case of the family, the resource and time deficits must not only be arrested, they must be reversed. For the community, the starting point is assuring the personal safety of our citizens, for the lack of safety in our communities has a formidable pull of its own. People forced to fear for their lives as they take an evening stroll are more inclined to take refuge in isolation than to go out and renew the community's infrastructure or spirit. Unless we root out this fear and violence, security will not be restored to communities. And finally, security for our country must start with a rethinking of the very term "national security," for there will be no security for our country or its citizens until we can offer opportunity to all by making capital accessible to the builders of business to create jobs for those who want and need them, and until we can equip men and women with the knowledge and skills they need to fill those jobs.

Working to assure these kinds of security has involved an all-out effort to connect the needs and resources among our giving areas, for their combined potential is considerable. A living example of this kind of synergy can be seen in Friendship Park. A year ago, Friendship Park was only an idea, but it was an idea backed by energy, funding and a group of people—many of them strangers to each other—who were determined to transform a rubble-strewn lot in Harlem into a place where community members could get together, play ball, have picnics and feel secure. The idea first came from a teacher at Rice High School, a school we have supported for years in its work with boys from disadvantaged backgrounds. Heather Bernard had little trouble galvanizing her students who had long looked out with disbelief on the wreckage of the adjacent lot, wondering not so much *what* could be done with it as *why* nothing had been done with it.

Early planning meetings included members of local churches and police precincts, block associations and the Urban League. Ever present was Guy Redding, a dedicated and long-time neighborhood resident who volunteered as park guardian. A grant from the Foundations of the Milken Families covered the bulk of the capital costs of the transformation, and the City of New York, through its Departments of Transportation and Parks, provided in-kind support to cover the balance.

Today, Friendship Park is a place that in every way fulfills its name. The place and the project have made friends out of strangers and a flourishing park out of a simmering problem. As one Rice student, Terrence Bailey, told us, "A place like this makes you believe that everything can change." Yes, it can. And what happened in Friendship Park will happen over and over again where concerned people have a clear vision and the determination to make it happen.

Because actual places can be so crucial to defining communities, we have worked to supply this kind of infrastructure in a number of different settings. Several years ago, we became involved in the Watts community—a severely stressed area in the southeastern part of Los Angeles—by helping to build the new Teen Center at the Westminster Neighborhood Association.

Watts has long been a community without a physical core, without even a single restaurant where families and friends could sit down and share a meal. We started working there because we know that people, whatever their age, do not get together in theory. They get together in fact. And for that to occur, they need a place. Our aim in building the Westminster Teen Center has not been to fix something that was wrong, but rather to promote healthy development for youngsters and their families by creating something the community needed but did not have, and the new center is doing that for a whole generation of local residents.

As is CHARO for the largely Latino population of East Los Angeles to whom it provides employment opportunities, training services and vocational rehabilitation for the handicapped. As is, too, in the western part of the San Fernando Valley, the Bernard Milken Jewish Community Campus that specifically supports family welfare through scores of educational, cultural and recreational programs for the very young, the very old and family members of every age between. And in the Crenshaw district of Los Angeles, we have focused on the equation of literacy and job opportunity, and, under the auspices of the Los Angeles Urban League, created a family literacy and education center. Again, the community is being fortified, but here, on the basis of individual victories over a notorious disability.

Though these centers create community in different ways, all of them embody our mission (Carnegie, 1993).[5] While our faith in one person's ability to make a large and lasting difference remains undiminished, we have a firm and active commitment to connecting individual efforts with one another, with appropriate institutional support and with the communities in which they take shape. Over the past year we have expanded our mission to include the commitment to developing our basic caregiving institutions. Working to fulfill that purpose has cast in sharp relief the importance of our focusing on the causes as distinct from the consequences of society's most debilitating ills.

The distinction between cause and consequence is, of course, a distinction between prevention and therapy. There are without question urgent human needs that must be met in the present; we continue our support of a select group of programs largely in the area of human welfare that work to alleviate acute deprivation and suffering. That these needs are the consequences of unmet deficits and unforestalled breakdowns in peoples' lives, however, simply underscores the need for focusing on their causes.

This shift in focus, gradual and steady, explains why the Foundations' support for education—always our primary concern—has grown over the last decade from 48 to 53 percent of all Foundation funding. It also points to why funding for community services, particularly as delivered by primary institutions, has remained steady, and why in 1992 approximately half of all health care and medical research funding was directed toward research. This shift is also why our investment in the Milken Institute for Job & Capital Formation is growing geometrically.

The Milken Institute precisely reflects the Foundations' commitment to investing in the security of our people, our communities and our country. Established with a mandate to support research into and discourse on the determinants of American economic growth, the Institute examines the policies and practices needed for meaningful employment opportunities and the means for assuring that we have qualified people to respond to those opportunities.

Key to the Institute's mission is its commitment to developing and maintaining a citizenry that is literate in economics. Our first of many planned conferences was held in October 1992 and brought together economists, businessmen and other community leaders to consider the topic "Economic Policy, Financial Markets and Economic Growth." The Institute has also launched an ambitious program to communicate the policy implications of its economic research not only to economists and business leaders but also to the general public by such means as documentary films and op-ed articles.

The Foundations' focus on investing in the human resources with which this country is so richly endowed is common to all the programs we have initiated, and each has received a steadily increasing percentage of Foundation funding over the years.

In education, we work in a number of areas, the largest of which supports the achievement and development of educators. It is the Milken Family Foundation National Educator Awards and Education Conference. Its aim has been—by means of financial recognition and professional development opportunities—to help restore education to its rightful place among professions and to attract talented and committed young people to the teaching profession, for if the future really is to belong to the educated, today's resources must be increasingly focused on those providing the education.

In the field of community services, we cultivate several kinds of development, and here, too, a significant share of our funding is directed to a program we created: the University-Community Outreach Program, better known as UCOP. Matching the human resources found on major urban universities with economic and educational development needs of the local community, UCOP has become a catalyst of basic institutional development in the four urban communities in which it is established. Of its many components, UCOP's core Young Entrepreneurs Program is a preventive investment of the first order, pairing high school students with MBA candidates as their mentors in a year-long program teaching them the ropes of entrepreneurship.

In the area of health care and medical research, among our largest commitments is the research award and grant programs we have established. We believe that basic and clinical research are the frontiers, far and near, of human investment; for visionary thinking can not only break through to new cures and therapies, it can trigger new thinking in others. It has been the Milken Family Medical Foundation's honor to add to this investment through our epilepsy and cancer research award programs that recognize the achievement of medial researchers with long and outstanding experience as well as the potential of especially promising younger scientists.

All festivals are celebrations, and the Festival for Youth and Holiday Toylift, our largest Foundation-initiated program in the area of human welfare, celebrates the greatest treasure there is—childhood. In fact, for many of the children touched by the Festival for Youth and Toylift, childhood is reawakened; for these are boys and girls who have known disadvantage as a way of life. In 1992, we reached more than 115,000 children. And, by taking them to circuses, ballgames and other special events during the spring and summer as well as by bringing them to celebrations and placing new toys in their hands at holiday time, it has been possible to show these children that they are neither alone nor forgotten.

Where there is a will—like Terrence Bailey's or Yvonne Chan's or that of countless others gathered for our Conferences—there is a way to plant a garden in concrete, to turn indifference into trust, to manage on one's own.

The challenges bearing down on our schools and educators are heavy, and they are complex, but they are not insoluble. To answer them, however, we must take hold of the responsibilities that have been severed from the basic institutions that for so long exercised them so efficiently and assign them to those institutions that can and will assume them. In this context, James Coleman sees society moving toward substituting informal institutions, such as the family, with formal organizations. It is precisely because our experience confirms that sober reading that we are committed to fortifying all our basic caregiving institutions, whatever their form, and to supporting the people who bring them to life.

Highlights of the 1993 Conference presented in this volume include Dr. Coleman's keynote remarks addressing the imperative of restoring society's basic institutions in terms of social capital, the theory he enunciated in the late 1980s. Taking the family as the most basic institution, Dr. Coleman focuses on its fragmentation and traces the separation of children from adults in three phases that have culminated in children's being "irrelevant." This is, of course, an intolerable alternative that can and must be replaced, as Coleman says, by the dynamic in which "the social and financial capital of one generation is invested in the creation of human capital in the next generation" (chapter 2, p. 23).

Joyce L. Epstein, a sociologist from Johns Hopkins and the Conference's second keynote speaker, underscores how important—and uncommon—it is for education to be geared to the coordinates of sociology, particularly those marking the intersection of schools, families and communities.

Explaining her preference for "partnership" to describe this juncture, Epstein points to the importance of shared responsibility, of parity among partners and of understanding that students are the fulcrum on which all of these arrangements balance.

Held to the light of special populations' needs, even more subtleties of the family/school/community connection are revealed. In the working part of the Conference, psychologist Diane Scott-Jones and education theorist Concha Delgado-Gaitan examine the role of family in children's development and schooling from African American and Spanish-speaking perspectives. Professor Annette Lareau takes a more critical approach as her research indicates the benefits of parental involvement are qualified by teachers' standards and parents' "social resources."

For an analysis of the actual implementation of family/school/community partnerships, the Conference turned to practitioners Pablo Perez, a long-time activist in developing such partnerships in the Mexican American communities of southern Texas, and Judy Daher, a deputy superintendent in California.

The Conference's closing panel, "The Media and the Schools," elicited sharply divergent views from the panelists and audience members alike. The Milken Institute for Job & Capital Formation has published a full report on the proceedings of that panel, including presentations by former *New York Times* education correspondent Edward Fiske, Nancy Perry of *Fortune* magazine, Thomas Toch, education correspondent of *U.S. News & World Report*, and Elaine Woo, of the *Los Angeles Times*.

* * *

The successful interaction of families, communities and schools is critical to the quality of education that children are equipped with as they face an exacting future. Because they guide our children, our country's educators are in direct touch with that future. And because they are educators, they have a responsibility to report back from that frontier. Diagnosis of and prescriptions for what ails American education issue from every quarter and from those who possess neither the experience nor the vision of the educators gathered at the National Education Conference. We need to know what our most talented teachers and principals are seeing in today's schools. We also need to know what they are thinking. Their commitment and their experience are not only a foundation upon which to build but a platform of credibility from which to speak out.

The battle has been joined, and some of the mightiest forces in the country are before us at the National Education Conference. The choice of arms, however, is limited to one—responsibility—responsibility for creating conditions within families, communities and schools that are worthy of our children.

As they confront the maelstrom of postmodern education, our nation's educators may feel beset, they may *be* beset, but they are not alone in their endeavor. We share their aspiration, and we are convinced it is attainable. Around us are communities prepared to be mobilized, parents ready to be enlisted, and children—needful and ardent—waiting for us to guide them into the secure future they deserve.

Notes

1. See chapter 2 for a thoughtful analysis of "Families in Crisis, Children in Jeopardy."

2. Consult Part One, "The Faces of Neglect," for an in-depth consideration of the effects on children of resource and time deficits.

3. The report, "The Demographics of American Families," commissioned by the Foundations of the Milken Families, offers detailed profiles of the many faces of American families today.

4. This is a thought-provoking brief on the need for and workings of a strong civic community.

5. *A Matter of Time: Risk and Opportunity in the Non-School Hours* is a comprehensive study of what today's young adolescents do, do not, and would benefit from doing with the vast majority of their time spent outside of school.

PART TWO

The Interaction of Schools, Families and Communities: An Overview

Introduction

Family involvement in children's education and community involvement in the schools can play fundamental roles in the success or failure of youth. In chapters two and three, the two keynote speakers at the Milken Family Foundation's National Education Conference in March of 1993—James Coleman and Joyce L. Epstein—address theoretical issues central to this book's concerns.

Family Involvement in Education

James Coleman is professor of sociology and education at the University of Chicago. His landmark study, *Equality of Educational Opportunity*, published in 1966, brought Coleman widespread recognition for ideas that were, at the very least, radically new and politically unacceptable for their time. Coleman's current research in part continues his studies of the functioning of schools and provides the basis for the chapter "Family Involvement in Education." Coleman reviews the changing roles of schools, community and family before focusing on the role schools and other social institutions can play in dealing with changes that have occurred in the family over the past century and a half.

Profound changes have impacted the family during this period with wide-ranging implications for children. In the early nineteenth century, in the most developed countries of the world, most families were engaged in "household production," that is, agriculture. With the Industrial Revolution, first men left the household for work outside it, then children enrolled in school, and finally, in the second half of the twentieth century, women left the household to work outside it.

Coleman's chapter describes this long-term change as involving an increase in "financial capital" directed toward the raising of children, combined with a decline in "social capital." (Coleman defines social capital as the involvement of adults in the family and the community in the lives of children.) Because financial capital is not a substitute for social capital in a child's development, the loss of social capital creates serious deficiencies in a child's social environment.

Coleman traces the radical change in the character of childhood over the past 150-200 years and the resulting changes in the character of schooling. At the beginning of this period, formal schooling hardly existed for most children. All activities and training that prepared children for adulthood took place within the household or within easy distance from it. Today, in highly developed countries, tangible school resources—financial investments in education—exist in over-supply in the school, in the home and generally throughout society. Social capital, however, is lacking. Interest in, time, effort, and attention invested in children now is not primary.

In this chapter, Coleman states that "the schools that are most effective in this . . . phase are those that are able to supply this social capital, to furnish the intangible qualities that compel students to take full advantage of the opportunities provided by the tangible resources" (p. 34). But school is not alone in competing for the interest and attention of children and there are dangers inherent in the erosion of social capital. One danger is that nothing will replace society's informal institutions. Today's children will therefore grow up in an environment of commercial recreation populated primarily by other children. Another danger, Coleman points out, is that old institutions will be replaced by "consciously designed ones" but ones inferior to those replaced.

Coleman, however, finds opportunity in the newly created institutions: The best of these will recognize that replacing lost social capital merely with greater "educational opportunities" is insufficient. Coleman calls these new institutions "analogous to the school"; however, they must fill "a more fundamental vacuum" by inducing the "kinds of motivations, attitudes and conception of self that children . . . need to succeed in school and as adults" (p. 37).

Family-School Partnerships

Chapter three is authored by Joyce L. Epstein, co-director of the Center on Families, Communities, Schools and Children's Learning and professor of sociology at The Johns Hopkins University. She has published extensively on the effects of schools, classrooms, family and peer environments on student learning and development and points to the major responsibilities the two institutions of family and school share in children's education. Epstein's research reported here concerns not just young children, but all children through the completion of schooling.

Epstein offers a framework for educators as they review present practices in developing comprehensive programs to involve school, family and community interaction. She begins by advancing the term "partnership" instead of the commonly used "involvement" to express the shared interests, responsibilities, investments and overlapping influences of families and school in the development and education of children. The broader term recognizes the school as equals in a partnership with families. It also recognizes the importance and potential influences of all family members—not only parents—and all family structures—not only those that include natural parents. Epstein's framework allows students, community organizations and individuals to join the partnership, "to invest in the education of the children whose futures affect the quality of life of the community" (p. 39).

The theoretical model Epstein discusses in chapter three is represented by what she calls "overlapping spheres of influence" (1987a), which include family, school, community and peer group, with students at the center of these overlapping spheres (1988). In Epstein's model, students are the main actors in their own success. Indeed, it is the school-family partnership that allows students to provide their own success. Epstein describes this partnership as one of "productive connections of schools and families" that helps students "increase their academic skills, self-esteem, positive attitudes toward learning, independence, other achievements, accomplishments and other desired behaviors that are characteristic of successful students" (p. 42).

Dr. Epstein enumerates six major types of involvement that create a comprehensive program of school-family partnerships:

- basic obligations of families including parenting skills and home conditions
- basic obligations of schools including communications about school programs and children's programs
- volunteers and audiences to support the school and students
- family involvement in learning activities at home
- participation by families in decision making, governance and advocacy
- collaboration with community groups and agencies to strengthen school programs, family practices and student learning and development.

It is important to note that not all types of involvement lead quickly or directly to achievement gains for students. Each of Epstein's types offers many variables, poses serious challenges and leads to different and significant outcomes. And, this framework is intended to work over a three- to five-year period. In addition to the theoretical model, Epstein's chapter offers examples of representative programs from selected states; these programs illustrate successful partnership practices in a variety of settings.

2

Family Involvement in Education

James S. Coleman

The character of childhood and youth has changed tremendously over the past two centuries, in ways that have extensive implications for the way children come into adulthood. Formal schooling hardly existed for most children and youth until this century. Children grew up in the context of the household and the neighborhood. All the activities and facilities for training that would prepare them for adulthood took place within the household or an easy distance from it. A child, as he or she grew, would slowly move into those activities with "training" being almost wholly confined to "on-the-job training," the job being agriculture, and it was closely linked to the household. For many children in the traditional sector of the third world that is still the way it is. The activities of the household and the village constitute their school.

This change is part of a long-term evolution involving an increase in financial capital directed toward the raising of children combined with a decline in social capital (where social capital can be regarded as the involvement of adults in the family and the community in the lives of children). But because financial capital and social capital are not substitutes for one another in a child's development, the loss of social capital for children and youth creates serious deficiencies in their social environments. There are ways in which these deficiencies can be overcome, some of which are outlined in the chapter.

We can ask what has happened over the past two centuries in the modern world to change the context of child-rearing from what it had been throughout history and prehistory. Some would describe it as a change in the locus of dominant activities in society. Until this century, the principal economic activities were within the household. The economy was a subsistence economy with families producing for their own use a far wider range of goods than they obtained by exchange, and most of what they obtained through exchange was from the local area. Even the most economic enterprises that employed other persons were outgrowths of household productions, had their basis in the family, and were located near to the family. One might say that the whole structure of social and economic organization had the family as its basic building block .

That changed, with the change accelerating from the latter half of the nineteenth century. The law recognized that change from an early period, defining a new kind of legal person: a "fictional person," as it was called, for it had no natural person as its head. It was *not* derivative from the household, but was a corporate body with a life of its own: free-floating in society, legally "owned" by a set of shareholders, but with a legal personality distinct from any of them. This new kind of person in society is the modern corporation. The French have an especially appropriate name for it, "societe anonyme," an anonymous society. I call it a corporate actor. The name is not important. What is important is that it is an actor in society; it does *not* derive from the family, and it has come to play an increasingly central role in the functioning of society.[1]

The growth of the corporation implied the removal of men's labor from the household and from close proximity to the household. Men left the farm or the neighborhood shop and went away to the office or the factory. An indicator of this change is the percentage of men in the labor force who are in agriculture. For agriculture is, or it was, the principal occupation that was carried out at home. Figure 2.1 shows the change in five now-industrialized countries: England, France, and Germany on the Continent and the United States and Canada in North America.

In the early to mid-nineteenth century, only England had less than a majority of men in agriculture. The other countries were strikingly similar, with a majority in agriculture until the late nineteenth century. This percentage has declined to a tiny fraction, five percent or less in the late-twentieth century. France, however, deviates in the middle period with a high proportion in agriculture until much later than the others.

The point of all this is that in these heavily industrialized countries of the world, most men's labor was still part of the household as late as a hundred years ago. The modern corporate actor, that is, the corporation, independent of the household as a locus for men's daily labor, is a relatively new condition for the main body of the population. A second change paralleled this movement of men out of the home: the growth of public schooling. As men ceased working in or near the home, there came to be a social investment in a new, "constructive" institution, the school. Although the complex of changes that led to public schooling cannot be easily separated, certainly the fathers leaving home-based employment where their sons could learn adult work from them for corporation-based employment was a non-trivial element of this. It is noteworthy

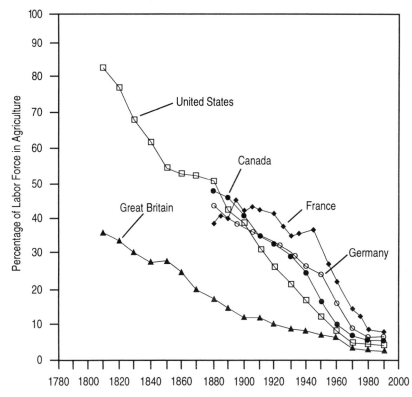

FIGURE 2.1 Data for France and Germany from the nineteenth century through 1975 and for Great Britain in 1961 and 1971 are taken from Peter Flora (1983, pp. 494, 512). Data for Great Britain from 1811 to 1951 are taken from Mitchell (1962, p. 60). Data for Canada from 1881 through 1951 are taken from Urquhart and Buckley (1965); for 1961 and 1971, from Statistics Canada (1976, Catalogue 94-175, Vol. 3). Data for the United States through 1970 taken from U.S. Bureau of the Census (1975, Tables, D167-181; 1990, Table 650). Data for all other countries for 1980 and 1987 are taken from United Nations (1990, Table 16).

that rural areas have always been the most resistant to compulsory schooling, and schools in rural areas have accommodated parental demands by dismissing school for planting or for harvesting.

The parallel growth of men's work outside the household and children being sent to school is shown for the United States in Figure 2.2. Along with the percentage of men in agriculture in the United States, which is taken from the first figure, Figure 2.2 shows the proportion of children and youth ages 5-19 who are not in school. From about 1850 on, this proportion corresponds closely to the proportion of men working in agriculture. The number of men on the farm and the number of children not in school decline together.

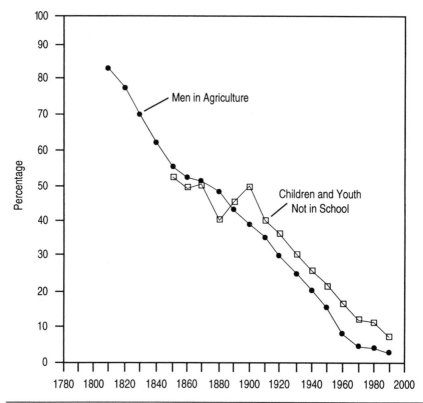

FIGURE 2.2 Data for men in agriculture are from U.S. Bureau of the Census (1975, Tables D167-181 for 1810 through 1860, Tables 11-25 for 1870–1970; 1990, Table 650, for 1980 and 1988). For 1810–1860, male and female labor force data are not reported separately. I have assumed that proportion of the male labor force in agriculture is approximately the same as proportion of total labor force in agriculture, an assumption that is correct for the next decade, 1870. Then, the percentage of total labor force in agriculture was 52.5, and the percentage of the male labor force in agriculture was 52.5. For children not in school, data are from U.S. Bureau of the Census (1975, Table II433-441; 1990, Table 214).

There have been extensive further changes from the period during which the corporation replaced the family in the father's daily life. One of the most striking has been the movement of women from the household to the corporation. Figure 2.3 shows, parallel to the percentage of men in agriculture, the percentage of women not in the paid labor force that are in the household during the day. The woman's movement out of the household parallels the man's movement out of the household about a hundred years later. The woman's presence in the household during the 1990s is just about like that of the man's in the 1890s.

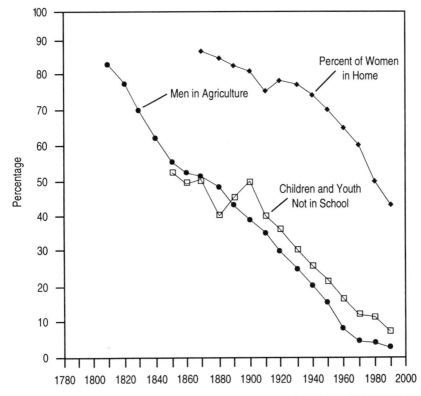

FIGURE 2.3 Data for men in agriculture are from U.S. Bureau of the Census (1975, Tables D167-181 for 1810 through 1860, Tables 11-25 for 1870–1970; 1990, Table 650, for 1980 and 1988). For 1810–1860, male and female labor force data are not reported separately. I have assumed that proportion of the male labor force in agriculture is approximately the same as proportion of total labor in agriculture, an assumption that is correct for the next decade, 1870. Then, the percentage of total labor force in agriculture was 52.5, and the percentage of the male labor force in agriculture was 52.5. For children not in school, data are from U.S. Bureau of the Census (1975, Table II433-441; 1990, Table 214). Data for women in home are from U.S. Bureau of the Census (1975, p. 128, Table D11-25; 1990, p. 378, Table 624).

As new corporate actors have swallowed up an increasingly large fraction of first men's and then women's activities and attention, the family has become a kind of irrelevant backwater in society cut off from the mainstream. But although this wall of corporate actors has come to be pervasive for adults, removing first fathers and then mothers from the household during the day, children remain outside this world.

This separation of children and adults often to worlds of their own can be seen as part of a long-term change in the relation of children and youth to adults. I will sketch what I see as three phases in this relation. These phases can be distinguished by their potential for investment in the human capital of the next generation. This investment in human capital occurs by applying the social and financial resources of adults toward the development of productive skills in children. *It can be quite simply described as the investment of the social and financial capital of one generation in the creation of human capital in the next generation.* The social capital consists of the social relationships within the family and community that generate the attention and the time that is spent by parents and community members in the development of children and youth. The financial capital consists of the monetary expenditures on formal institutions designed toward that same goal. The principal such institution is, of course, the school.

Phase 1: The Exploitation of Children's Labor

A household in Phase 1 is a household living near a subsistence level. A Phase 1 economy is one in which most households are near a subsistence level. An economy based largely on subsistence farming is the most widespread example, though extractive economies in general, in which most occupations are in the primary economic sector, fit this phase. Village-based societies in which most households are engaged in herding also fit here. In such social structures, households directly produce most of what they consume; economic exchange and division of labor are minimal.

In such societies the household is a principal productive institution. The household has both responsibilities for its children and authority over the children. In economists' terms, property rights over children are vested in the family.[2] The labor of children is useful to the household both because in the diversified activities of the household there are always tasks that children can carry out and because the economic level of the household is sufficiently low that the effort of everyone is needed. The cost of children to the family in this phase is low because food is ordinarily produced at home. Families exercise their property rights in children through having many children and then exploiting their capacity for labor with little regard for the impact of this upon the children's opportunities. Such societies are ordinarily stable over generations and there is little of what in modern society can be described as "opportunity." Families have a narrow horizon, are inwardly focused, and have little interest in the resources for extending their children's horizons broadly. In this stage the family makes very little financial investment in its children beyond that implicit in the "on-the-job" training the child gets through labor in the household or in apprenticeship in a nearby household. The family's investments of social capital consist primarily of the informal social resources of family and proximate community members and are directed to short-term payoffs in the productivity of their children. Long-term investments are limited because the family requires productive activity from the young as soon as they are able. Formal schooling is hardly necessary, and, for societies at this stage, schools are scarce. This can be seen in Figure 2.2, which shows the proportion of children and youth ages 5-19 in the United States in 1990 who are not in school. The fact that the proportion not in school closely tracks the proportion of men in agriculture is suggestive evidence of the irrelevance of formal schooling for raising children in stable subsistence farming societies.

Phase 2: Children as Investments for the Family

A post-agricultural, urban, industrial society engaged largely in manufacturing and some commerce defines Phase 2. Here the economy is an exchange economy. Most labor is performed in full-time jobs and the family's economic needs are provided mainly through the exchange of wages for goods. Children's labor is no longer needed for the household's economy and there are fewer possibilities for productive work of children within the household. In such a society, and even in the movement from Phase 1 to Phase 2, opportunity for the young begins to take on meaning. In such a society the family continues to have a strong interest in children but now for a more long-range goal. The family retains its implicit property rights in its children, in part as a residue from Phase 1. Families are still the central institutions of society, again, in part as a residue from this first phase. Although the household is no longer the principal locus of production in this society, the full implications of this have not been realized because the family retains many related functions. The family's "interests" are still closely linked to each of its member's interests.

Children are the carriers of the family across generations from the past into the future, and parents' investment in children is an investment in the human capital for their old age as well as for the family's future. A large number of children is no longer valuable for this latter purpose, but high investments made in each child, that is, to increase the status position and the economic position and the social respectability of the family in the next generation, are of value.

It is especially important to recognize two points about this phase—points that are relevant to the problems that young people face today. The first is that the productive capacity of a family's children is important to the family's future, both for the parents' own well-being in the dependency of old age and for the well-being of the family as a corporate body extending over generations. Second, the value of the child to the family is not in terms of current production but in terms of its future productive capacity.

The first of these two points implies that the family has a direct material interest in developing its children's productive capacity. Investments in the child's education and skill development are not merely investments in the child's future welfare; they are investments for the parents' future welfare as well and for the family's standing in the community.[3] The second point implies that the family's interest in future productivity over the whole course of adulthood rather than immediate benefits is the case and is not what is true in Phase 1. The two points taken together imply that the family will have a strong material interest in the child's welfare, a material interest that coincides largely with the child's own long-range interest. Exploitation of the child is no longer in the family's interest if it will reduce the child's future productive potential. Investment in the child is in the family's interest.

A demographer, John Caldwell, has characterized this transition from exploitation to investment as a change in the direction in the flow of wealth. Before the change, Caldwell (1976) says the flow was from the younger generation to the older one, backward. After the change, the flow was from the older generation to the younger one, forward. Phase 2 is associated with social change, especially beginning with the Industrial Revolution. This implies not only that the family can afford investments in the future but also that the social resources in the family and its immediate environment are not sufficient and even not appropriate for the skills the young will need. Financial investments in training for the young are necessary and these investments are primarily in a specialized institution, that is, the school. Schooling of the child comes to be important to the family.

This can be seen especially well in Europe, where many families left the first phase only after World War II. Before that time, secondary education was not universal; a large portion of the population gained employment immediately after elementary school. After 1945, a strong demand for equal educational opportunity was created, secondary education became universal, and, in the 1960s, there arose a demand to replace the two-tiered secondary educational system with comprehensive schools enrolling all youth in the community.

Phase 2 is a transitional phase as suggested by the earlier point. The centrality of the family exists in part as a residue with its functional strength in the first phase. Over time this residue comes to be washed away, and the connection of individual interests to family interest is weakened. In developing societies, the second phase in the relationship of youth to society has begun to be replaced by a third phase.

Phase 3: Children as Irrelevant

Phase 3 is an advanced industrial society, or, what Daniel Bell (1973) has called a postindustrial society, or a welfare state with a high degree of affluence. In this phase the family's central role in the economy has vanished, and the family itself has become a kind of appendage to the economic structure. It is an institution relevant to consumption that is no longer important to production. Its functional role has been reduced to that of child rearing.

The family's central place in the economy and in society has been taken over by large and small corporate bodies, industrial and commercial corporations. When the economic functions of the household are siphoned off to other institutions, the family can retain its raison d'être only for a period of time. It is no longer an institution spanning lifetimes but one that forms anew with each successive generation. Its interest in children to carry the family into the future declines. The stability of marriages and thus of households declines. The extended family is no longer able to restrain its members from choosing individualistic solutions at the expense of the family.

Other changes in advanced societies are also consistent with the irrelevance of children in Phase 3. More couples choose not to have children. Leisure activities take place increasingly in age-segregated settings exemplified by cocktail parties for the adults and rock concerts for the young. The gulf between adults in their work institutions and youth in their educational institutions has increased.

As the above discussion indicates, the potential for investment in the next generation changes as society itself changes. If we think of investments in youth as investments in the next generation's human capital, it is useful to distinguish investments of two kinds. First, time, effort, and attention of adults in the family and in the informal community surrounding the family—what I earlier described as investments of social capital; and, second, investments through the employment of professionals and formal organizations, in particular, schools are distinct. I have described these as investments of financial capital.

The relations as I have described them, between the investments of social capital and the investments of financial capital in the human capital of the next generation, can be described schematically (see Figure 2.4). This figure shows the continually increasing investment of financial capital in the creation of human capital, and the equally continually *decreasing* investment of social capital. The increasing investment of financial capital is

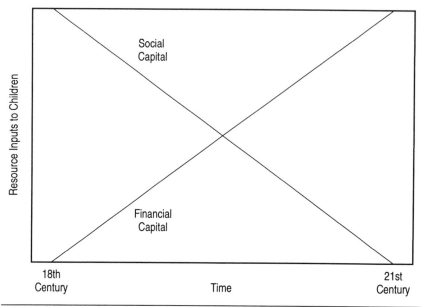

FIGURE 2.4

a direct consequence of economic development. Such growth leads to an increase in the affluence of the society and of the families in the society. The decreasing investment in social capital reflects an indirect consequence of that same economic development. The family, a specialized institution in an exchange economy, is less likely to be a place where the everyday activities lead toward a focus on developing productive skills.

There are various ways in which the investment of financial capital and social capital might combine to produce human capital in the young. If the human capital product was merely the sum of two types of investments, that is, if one, financial capital, was perfectly substitutable for the other, that is, social capital, then that would be one kind of combination. However, Figure 2.5 shows the human capital produced if the two types investments combined in a different way, that is, combined in what we might say is "multiplicatively." This multiplicative output is limited by the lower of the two investment lines. It is limited by financial investment on the left and limited by social investment on the right. The result is that the overall human capital produced is highest in this middle period and not in the latter period.

There is evidence that I will not go into, especially that comparing less developed countries with more developed countries, which indicates that financial capital (expressed principally through investments in

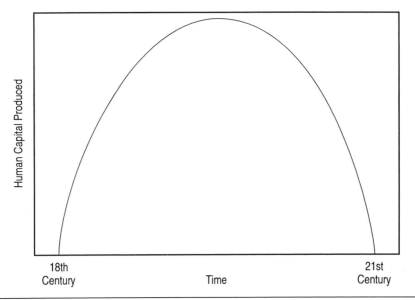

FIGURE 2.5

formal schooling) is not a perfect substitute for social capital as exemplified by family and community (Schneider and Coleman, 1993). Substantively, this suggests that two different kinds of resources are necessary for the growth of human capital: the existence of educational opportunities (through the investments of financial capital, primarily in the school but in other institutions as well), and the presence of motivation and interest (a result of the investment of social capital primarily in the family and the community). If either one of these is missing, these opportunities will not be available and human capital development will be blocked. This implies that the production function in education is something like the multiplicative function that I have indicated.

Returning to Figure 2.4, human capital development is blocked or impeded in the first phase, what I have described as the eighteenth century, by a lack of financial capital. It is blocked or impeded in the third phase, what I have called the twenty-first century, resulting from a deficiency of social capital. In Phase 1, financial capital is in short supply and constitutes what might be called the "limiting factor." In Phase 3, the limiting factor is declining social capital. This implies that in Phase 1 an increase in finances for education will make great differences in human capital development. In Phase 3, an increase in the social capital provided by family and community would have a comparable effect.

If this picture is correct, highly developed countries are currently moving into the third phase, a phase in which tangible school resources—financial investments in education—are in over-supply, not only in the school itself but also in the home and quite generally throughout society. Social capital—the motivations that strong families interested in investing time, effort, and attention in their children provided in Phase 2—are lacking in Phase 3, however. The schools that are most effective in this third phase are those able to supply this social capital, to furnish the intangible qualities that impel students to take advantage of the opportunities that are provided by the tangible resources. The school in Phase 3 is one of the many elements competing for the attention and interest of a child or youth, and what cannot be taken for granted in this phase are the motivational forces that direct attention and interest toward learning rather than toward other attractive competitors for the child's or youth's attention and interest.

What I have tried to do is to give a partial diagnosis of the problems of bringing children and youth into adulthood in modern society, or, as an economist might put it, the problems of developing human capital in the next generation. I have argued that the growth of human capital requires investments not only of financial capital but also social capital. I have argued also that parents who in Phase 2 of society's developments made those investments, now in Phase 3 have far fewer incentives for doing so.

The arguments from the preceding section imply that these incentives have been destroyed by the weakening of the family. The social capital, as reflected by the presence of adults in the home and the range of exchange between parents and children about academic, social, economic and personal matters, has declined. At the same time, the parents' human capital, their own human capital, has grown.

In the community outside the family, the erosion of social capital in the form of effective forms of social control or adult-sponsored youth organizations and informal relations between children and youth has been even greater. The earlier migration of fathers from the household and the neighborhood during the day and the very recent migration of mothers from the household into the labor force has meant reduced participation in community organizations like PTA, scouting and others. In addition, the society has been invaded by an advanced individualism in which cultivation of one's own well-being has replaced interest in others. Indicators of this are the extensive growth and concern with one's health through jogging and health clubs and so on.

Altogether, the social capital in family and neighborhood available for raising children has declined precipitously. The cost, of course, will be borne by the next generation and borne disproportionately by the disadvantaged of the next generation, for the loss of social capital in the community hurts most the children with least human and social capital in the family.

All this would not matter, of course, in a society in which social capital was abundant. In the past, many persons struggled to escape the social norms of an oppressive, closely-knit community. But the world has changed. In the individualistic present, each person narcissistically attends to self-development with little attention leftover for children, certainly not for others' children. It is very likely a reaction to this absence of community social capital which has led many inner-city African American parents to send their children to Catholic schools and other African American parents to establish with a few friends small ad hoc private schools. It is very likely a reaction to these same social changes that has led to the conservative Christian school movement, a movement in which parents are striving to re-create for their children's upbringing some of the social capital that once existed in local neighborhoods but does so no longer.

These are private responses. We may ask what in the public policy domain are implications of the social changes that have resulted in a loss of social capital for the family and outside it.

Public Investments in Social Capital

The loss of social capital inside and outside the family has extensive implications for the structure of American child rearing. Raising children once took place informally as a by-product of other activities in social institutions, that is, the household, the extended family, and the neighborhood-based organizations that were held in place by these other activities. As the locus of the other activities has changed, the institutions have crumbled and the by-product, raising children, has crumbled along with them. The institutions that have replaced them—the offices and factories replacing household or neighborhood as work places; shopping malls and catalogs replacing neighborhood stores as places to shop; cocktail parties and rock concerts replacing gatherings of extended families at leisure settings—are inhospitable to the relations between adults and children that constitute the social capital for children's growth.

This wholesale destruction of institutional "underbrush" of society brings both dangers and opportunity. One danger lies in the possibility that nothing will replace these informal institutions and children will grow up in an environment consisting primarily of commercial recreation, music, clothes and thrill-generating activities, and populated primarily by other children. The opportunity lies in the possibility that new institutions designed expressly for child rearing can do so better than a system in which most child rearing occurred as a by-product.

To realize the opportunity rather than the danger, it is valuable to re-call history. When men left the household in great numbers for daily work outside it in the late nineteenth and early twentieth centuries, an extensive public investment was made in mass public schooling. One might suggest that this was designed to replace the informal social cap-ital that became unavailable to children when the father left the house-hold for factory or office.

A second major transformation of the household is now occurring, of perhaps even greater magnitude in the lives of children, as the woman leaves the household for the factory or the office and as the neighbor-hood declines in strength. The parallel suggests a similar replacement of informal social capital as a by-product of other activities with the formal institution analogous to or part of the school.

The general shape of the demand for a new institution is clear: It is a demand not for further classroom activities, not for further classroom in-doctrination, nor for any particular content, but a demand for child care. It is a demand for care, first, all day from birth to school age; second, after school every day until parents return from work; and, third, all summer.

It is important, however, to look at something more than the explicit demand, because merely meeting the demand of parents may satisfy their needs without replacing the social capital that is important for chil-dren. Two points must be recognized: first, the outputs of education—the motivation and interest—with qualities of the school. As the social capital in the home and background shrinks, school achievement and other growth will not be increased by replacing these resources with more school-like resources—that is, those that produce "educational op-portunities"—but rather by replacing them with resources that produce motivation and interest, that is, those qualities that interacted with ones that have traditionally been provided by the school.

The second point is that some indication of what those resources must be like can be seen in the character of the currently eroding institutions that have provided this social capital in the past. Their essential qualities have been, I believe, attention, personal interest, an intensity of involve-ment, some persistence and continuity over time, and a certain degree of intimacy.[4] Beyond these few statements about the nature of investments in social capital for the next generation to bring the greatest benefit, I am not prepared to go. But several points are clear. As we move toward a new structure of the household and neighborhood in which many of the activities that provided human capital for the next generation are no longer present, new investments in social capital are both in demand and socially desirable. These new institutions are analogous to the school, in that the demand for them arises as the mother leaves the household, just as a demand for mass schooling arose as the father left the household. Yet, they cannot be exactly like the school traditionally has been in the kinds of qualities they engender in children. For the social capital that is now eroding leaves a more fundamental vacuum. They must be institutions that induce the kinds of motivations, the kinds of attitudes, and the conception of self which children and youth will need to succeed in school and as adults.

Notes

1. A major difference between the Japanese corporation and that of Europe and America is that in the transition from feudalism to capitalism in Japan, the noble household remained more fully unscathed by revolution than in the West, and it served as the basis for the highly paternalistic Japanese corporation. Many welfare activities that are the province of the state in the West are the province of the corporation in Japan.

2. Vivid descriptions of such households in seventeenth century America can be found in Demos (1970). For characterization of English households at about the same time, see Laslett (1971). Laslett (1972) gives some information about households and the treatment of children throughout Europe, although the focus is primarily demographic.

3. There may still be under investment in the child's educational development because the parent captures only a part of the benefits of that education. The situation is like that of a firm investing in the creation of human capital in its employees, largely specific human capital (benefits captured by the firm) but with some general human capital (benefits not captured by the firm) as well. To the extent that the general human capital is inextricably bound with the specific human capital, the firm, not able to capture all the benefits, will under invest (see Becker, 1964).

4. Such institutions carry dangers, particularly those of sexual exploitation of children by adults. In the family this danger is held at bay by the incest taboo, though this taboo weakens in single-parent families with complex custodial and visiting arrangements. Institutions like YMCA and boarding schools have always had to find sanctions to contain homosexuality, and some similar devices are necessary for any newly-constructed institutions.

3

Theory to Practice: School and Family Partnerships Lead to School Improvement and Student Success

Joyce L. Epstein

The Milken Family Foundation's National Education Conference offers a forum for discussion on the sociology of education, and that in education is a rarity. It is a rarity for educators to have an opportunity to think about how sociology contributes to our thinking about schools, families and communities. What follows, then, is a discussion about how we think about, how we talk about, and how we act to produce school, family, and community partnerships.

The Concept of "Partnership"

The term "school, family, and community partnerships" is a better, broader term than "parent involvement" to express the shared interests, responsibilities, investments, and the overlapping influences of family, school and community for the education and development of the children they share across the school years. The broader term emphasizes that the institutions share the major responsibilities for children's education and development and that all—school, family and community—are needed to support children as students. In addition to recognizing the school as an equal in the partnership, the broader term recognizes the important potential influence of all family members, not just parents, and all family structures, not just natural parents. Moreover, the term allows students to join the partnership as communicators with and for their own families and schools. The term makes room, too, for community groups, individuals, agencies and organizations to work with schools and families to invest in the education of children whose futures affect the quality of life of the community, of the family, and of the child.

Partnership is a word that encompasses many of the themes about "capital" referred to in Coleman's and Milken's chapters. We *take stock* in our partnerships; we account for our *resources* and *investments*, and we look for *profits* for all concerned. Thus I choose to emphasize the word partnership for this discussion about school, family and community connections.

Theoretical Model: Overlapping Spheres of Influence

The term "partnership" is represented in a theoretical model that I call "overlapping spheres of influence" (Epstein, 1987a, 1992). The spheres of influence on children's learning and development include the family and the school, or, in full form, the family, school, community and peer group. The spheres can, by design, be pushed together to overlap to create an area for partnership activities, or pushed apart to separate the family and school based on forces that operate in each environment. The external model of the spheres of influence shows that the extent of overlap is affected by forces of (a) time, to account for changes in age and grade levels of students and the influence of historic changes, and (b) efforts and behavior to account for the backgrounds, philosophies and practices that occur in each environment. The *external model* recognizes pictorially that there are some practices that schools and families (and other spheres) conduct separately and some practices that they conduct jointly in order to influence children's learning and development.

We know that in many schools there still are educators who say, "If the family would just do its job, we could do our job." That wording represents a view of "separate spheres of influence." In effect, these people are saying, "Let's separate the family and the school in order to have the most efficient organizations possible. If the family carries out its mission, we'll all do very well, thank you." In other, more complicated words, this has been the prevailing theory in sociology from the turn of the century until approximately the mid-1970s (Waller, 1932; Weber, 1947; Parsons, 1959). As we began to study school and family partnerships, we found that the theory of separate spheres was not useful for explaining the effective organization of education for children. Rather, our data suggested the need to push the spheres together so that they overlap somewhat, as shown in Figure 3.1. This picture recognizes that the school and the family *share* their children (Epstein, 1987a). All the years the children attend school, they attend home. Regardless of family structure or economic conditions, families send the best children they have to school, and educators send them home again.

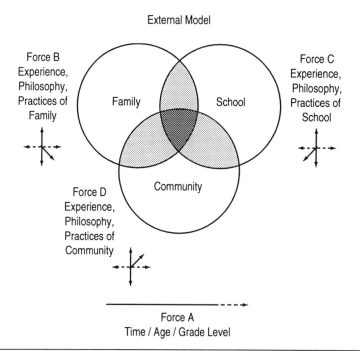

FIGURE 3.1 Overlapping Spheres of Influence of Family, School and Community on Children's Learning. *Source:* Epstein, 1987a, 1992

The *internal model* of the spheres of influence, shown in detail in Figure 3.2, recognizes the influence of the complex and essential interpersonal relations and influence patterns that occur between and among individuals at home and at school in practices that concern students' education and development. The same connections could be drawn for the full model of interactions of family, school, community and peer group. There are two levels of interpersonal relations and exchanges that represent different practices that we work on as we develop partnerships. One occurs at the *institutional level*, such as when a school invites all families to an event or sends the same communications to all families. In Figure 3.2, the letters F and S, for Family and School designate a general or common practice to involve all families in a school. The second level of interactions occurs at the *individual level*, as when a parent, teacher, or student meet in conference to discuss an individual student's progress or problem, or when a teacher telephones or writes to a parent for an individual communication.

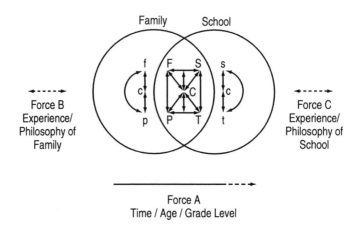

FIGURE 3.2 Overlapping Spheres of Influence of Family, School and Community on Children's Learning. *Source:* Epstein, 1987a, 1992

In Figure 3.2, all of the arrows intersect at the very center of the picture, at the letter C, for child. It is this "central role of the student" that is the reason we talk about partnerships. Students are at the center of the model of overlapping spheres of influence for school, family and community partnerships. They are the main actors in their education, development, and success in school. School and family partnerships do not "produce" successful students. Rather, the partnership activities that include teachers, parents, and students engage, guide, energize, and motivate students so that *they* produce their own success. The model assumes that student learning, development, and success, broadly defined—not just achievement test scores—are the main reasons for school and family partnerships. Further, productive connections of schools, families and communities, and pertinent individual interactions of teachers, parents, and students are conducted in order to help students increase their academic skills, self-esteem, positive attitudes toward learning, independence, other achievements, talents, accomplishments, and other desired behaviors that are characteristic of successful students. Figure 3.2 shows the social exchanges that can, through good design of programs and practices, produce the human and social capital that we want to result from school and family partnerships.

Six Major Types of Involvement

If we say that schools and families overlap in their responsibilities, what practices of partnership should occur in those areas of overlap? How can educators design a program that represents the model shown in Figures 3.1 and 3.2? Our research since 1980 has provided a good deal of information about how we think good practices of partnership can be developed in every school. Our data has led us to create a framework of six major types of partnership activities to form a comprehensive program of school, family, and community partnerships. The six types of involvement that form a comprehensive program of partnership are not unfamiliar to many practitioners. As we review the types of involvement I ask you to ask yourselves, "Do we do this at our school? How do we do it? With which families do we do this? And, how well does this work at our school?"

Figure 3.3, entitled Type 1, refers to the basic obligations of families. It is what families do when people say, "If the family would just do its job!" This includes the basic levels of support for health and safety, nutrition, housing, parenting skills and child rearing that are the parents' jobs across the grades. Particularly important are families' activities to establish positive home conditions that support their children's learning and behavior across all the school years. Schools usually assist families to develop this knowledge by organizing family support programs and by running workshops. Topics may include, for example, How to be a parent of a successful first grader or fourth grader, What is a middle school? What is an early adolescent? How to discipline a middle school child, How to prevent drug abuse, and so on. These kinds of workshops help parents understand their obligations, parenting skills, and home conditions for learning all across the school years.

• Housing, Health, Nutrition, Safety

• Parenting Skills and Child Rearing for all Age Levels

• Home Conditions for Learning at all Grade Levels

FIGURE 3.3 Type 1—Basic Obligations of Parents. *Source:* Epstein, 1992

For each of the six types of involvement in the partnership model there are "challenges." A challenge is an educator's euphemism for "problem." The challenges must be overcome to successfully produce each type of partnership, and to create social connections and exchanges that work. One challenge for Type 1 is that once a workshop for parents is planned, refreshments delivered, and an expert speaker engaged, only 6 or 13 people show up! We conducted a large survey of parents to find out when parents are able to come to school (Epstein, 1986). Of the total respondents, about one fourth said the morning, one fourth replied the afternoon, and the rest answered the evening hours. If you factor in the topic of the workshop and other variables that affect people's time and interests, your equation would predict that 6-13 parents would show up.

This does not mean that schools should stop conducting workshops to fulfill Type 1 to help parents understand their basic obligations for parenting at each grade level. Rather, they need to use the technology of the 1990s and into the twenty-first century to help all parents who cannot come to the workshop at that hour on that day to get the information in forms and in languages that they can understand, and in ways they can access the information. For example, a videotape of a workshop can be seen at school at any time of the day. That video becomes a part of the school's video library on parenting skills and home conditions for learning. Or, the information from the workshop may be offered in a tape recording that can be borrowed, or in a written summary, or via a computerized phone line that parents can call to hear a summary of the main parts of the workshop. Schools need to be innovative and technologically alert to overcome the challenges of Type 1 and to help all families at each grade level understand how they can build home conditions to support their children as students across the years.

The next figure explains Type 2—the basic obligations of schools to effectively communicate with families about school programs and children's progress. Communications include notices, calls, report cards, conferences, memos, and other information that all parents receive during a school year. It includes the information to help families choose or change schools, if that is an option; or to help families help students select curricula, courses, special programs and activities.

Schools vary the forms and frequency of these communications. They also vary the media in which these communications are delivered to all parents. Schools expect families to respond or to react knowledgeably to these communications. There are, of course, some challenges associated with Type 2 communications. In one middle school, for example, we found that only 33 percent of the newsletters made it home (Epstein and Herrick, 1991). The other 67 percent were decorating the city of Baltimore. Another example of a Type 2 challenge concerns conferences.

• **School-to-Home**

Memos, Notices, Newsletters, Report Cards,
Conferences, Phone Calls

Information to Help Choose or Change Schools

Choose or Change Courses, Placements, Programs, Activities
and other Opportunities

Other Innovative Communications on School Programs
and Student Progress

• **Home-to-School**

Two-Way Channels for Interaction and Exchange

FIGURE 3.4 Type 2—Basic Obligations of Schools Communications. *Source:* Epstein, 1992

Parent-teacher conference schedules must reflect the fact that over two thirds of the mothers of children in a school may work full or part-time during the school day (Epstein, 1986). As a third example, if report cards go home with no explanation of how grades are earned or how grades can be improved, then educators cannot complain that families are not being responsive to students' problems. If schools communicate with families, the information must not only get home, but also must be understood by all families. That means it must be written in the languages and vocabularies that all families can read or access.

In our surveys of elementary, middle, and high school teachers, parents, and (at the high school level) students, we found that parents are very eager for this information (Epstein, 1986; Dauber and Epstein, 1993; Connors and Epstein, 1994). Parents at all economic levels, in all communities—urban, rural and suburban—are asking, "How do I help? What can I do? Where is the information I need?" When children are infants or young toddlers, a variety of places offer families information about early growth and development, and about parental duties and responsibilities. This information becomes more complex and more difficult to acquire as children go from elementary to middle to high school grades. School, family, and community partnerships can assure that information flows in both directions: school information to home and family information to school.

Type 3 in my framework is involvement at the school building, as shown in Figure 3.5. Schools can improve their outreach and vary their schedules so that more families are recruited and are able to volunteer; so that they match volunteers' skills, talents, and time to teachers' and students' needs. Volunteers may include all families, not just well-educated families. We listen to families who say, "I'm home during the school day, but I didn't know I was welcome to come to volunteer." Or, "I would like to volunteer, but they don't seem to welcome me there." Some potential volunteers are turned away when they call the school and talk with a secretary who may not have been informed about or included in plans to increase parent and community volunteers. We need to develop volunteer programs to accept the challenge to vary schedules so that families can volunteer at different times during the school day, and so that school assemblies or sports events are not scheduled only at one time of the day or evening. Schools can be more "family friendly" about these things.

Another Type 3 challenge is to change the definition of "volunteer" to be "anybody, anytime, any place, who supports school goals or children's learning." That would open up many opportunities to recognize volunteers who participate at home and in the community, as well as those who come to school during the school day. Some private schools allow volunteers to work in the evenings, on weekends, on business holidays (as

---

• Volunteers

  In School or Classroom
    To assist administrators, teachers, students or parents
    (includes mentors, coaches, boosters, monitors, chaperones,
    tutors, lectures, leaders, demonstrators and other roles)

  For School or Classroom
    To assist school programs or children's progress from
    any location

• Audiences

  Assemblies, Performances, Sports Events, Recognitions and
  Awards, Celebrations, Other School or Classroom Events

FIGURE 3.5 Type 3—Involvement at School. *Source:* Epstein, 1992

distinct from school holidays) and in the summer. The number of volunteers can be increased by broadening the definition of volunteers and arranging more inclusive processes for volunteering.

The next type of involvement—Type 4—refers to family involvement in learning activities at home, as reported in Figure 3.6. A large part of my research efforts have focused on this type. It may be the hardest type to implement because it requires every teacher to recognize the connection between the child in the classroom, the curriculum of the school, and the family's connection to the child as a learner at home. Most parents say they want answers to the question: "How do I help my child this year do better in school?" Although only some parents want to be involved at the school building as volunteers or in leadership roles, just about all want to know what they can do at home each year to help their child do better in school.

One Type 4 challenge is for teachers to overcome some inaccurate ideas about family involvement in homework and other learning activities at home. Some teachers consider this type of involvement and ask, "Does that mean that I have to teach every parent of every child in my room how to teach every subject?" Fortunately, Type 4 does *not* mean this.

The saying "Parents are their children's first and most important teacher" is true. But this axiom does mean that parents want to teach their children the curriculum of the school. Parents are not asking, "How do I teach my fifth grader fractions?" or, "How do I teach my seventh grader science?" Our research with thousands of parents has shown that parents want to motivate, encourage, monitor, keep track of, interact with, and talk about school work at home. They want to be knowledgeable partners, not teachers of all curricula (Epstein, 1986; Dauber and Epstein, 1993; Connors and Epstein, 1994).

- Required Skills to Pass Each Grade

- How to Help at Home on Homework
  (monitoring, discussing, interacting, helping, following-up)

- Curriculum-Related Decisions

- Other Skills and Talents

FIGURE 3.6 Type 4—Involvement in Learning Activities at Home. *Source:* Epstein, 1992

Parents have been told to ask their child everyday, "How was school today?" Students usually answer "O.K." or "good" or "Ugh." Schools must help parents move beyond this relatively unprovocative question in order to engage their children in discussions about learning. Students need to know that Mom thinks math is important and interesting, that science is all around them, that social studies links to something that their parents, grandparents, or great grandparents did in earlier times, that English writing is something everyone does to communicate, and that people at home are interested in hearing a paragraph or story they write for school.

These kinds of interactions with their children enable parents to stay informed and to be involved in their children's learning. To help teachers improve their communications with parents in Type 4, we developed an interactive homework process called Teachers Involve Parents in Schoolwork, or TIPS (Epstein, Jackson and Salinas, 1992). Simply put, for TIPS, teachers design homework that requires children to talk to someone at home about something interesting they are learning in class. This takes place on a regular, systematic basis, perhaps weekly or biweekly. With TIPS, the child is the "interacter," the interviewer, the demonstrator of a new skill learned in school. The parent is the listener, reactor, or is asked to share ideas. For example, a middle grades science homework activity asks students to conduct an experiment and discuss osmosis at home. TIPS puts school on the agenda at home with activities that promote thinking, stimulate interest, improve the design of homework, and have a chance of increasing student success in school by improving their homework completion, weekly tests, and report card grades. There are TIPS program manuals for teachers and prototype activities to help elementary and middle grades educators use this process.

A high school TIPS program is in its early stages. Some believe high school students do not wish to recognize let alone talk with a parent at home. We surveyed ninth graders in six urban, rural, and suburban high schools during the first quarter of 1993 (Epstein, Connors and Salinas, 1993). Students checked the activities they were willing to do at home if their teacher asked them to do so. They overwhelmingly agreed that they could: interview my parent, interview some family member, talk with a person in the community about interesting things we are doing in school, and get some reactions to them. These are the kinds of interactions that keep a dialogue going at home about school. Conversations like these are important to assure that children of all ages come to school knowing that someone at home thinks school is worth the students' time and efforts. And, these interactions bring the students into the school and family partnership.

* **PTA/PTO**
  (Membership, Participation, Representation, Leadership)

* **Advisory Councils and Committees**

  School Improvement, Chapter 1, School-Site Management and Others

* **Independent School Advocacy Groups**

FIGURE 3.7 Type 5—Decision Making, Participation, Leadership and School Advocacy.
Source: Epstein, 1992

The fifth type of involvement, shown in Figure 3.7, is decision making, participation, leadership and school advocacy. Activities in this type involve parents in committees, PTA, PTO, school-site management teams and school-based decision-making teams. There are numerous efforts across this country to bring the voices of parents into school decision making and school improvement activities that affect their children. One challenge for success with Type 5 is to correct problems of lack of representation of some groups of parents. In some schools there is very little input from parents to their representatives, and there is very little return of information to parents from their parent-leaders. As an example, in one school we visited in California, 80 percent of the children were Hispanic, 20 percent Anglo, but just about all of the parent representatives and committee members were from Anglo families. A new principal came to that school, saw the situation as unacceptable, and over a four- or five-year period was able to alter the percentage of participation to about 50 percent Anglo, 50 percent Hispanic representation. And, he and the parents were still working on the issue as of the summer of 1992.

The last type of involvement, Type 6, concerns collaborations and exchanges with the community (see Figure 3.8). These are the connections that enable the community to contribute to schools, students, and families. These also include connections that students make to serve others in their community. There is a growing interest in this type of partnership as can be seen in other chapters throughout this volume. School partnerships with individuals and institutions in the community can assist all children, strengthen school programs, and improve the connections that families make to resources and services in their community.

• **Connections to Enable the Community to Contribute to Schools, Students and Families**

Businesses, Agencies, Cultural Groups, Health Services, Recreation

Other Groups and Programs to Improve and Enrich School Programs and Student Learning and Family Strengths

• **Connections to Enable Schools, Students and Families to Contribute to the Community**

FIGURE 3.7 Type 6—Collaborations and Exchanges with the Community. *Source:* Epstein, 1992

We recently conducted a survey of high school students and asked the students if they participated in a school-business partnership (Epstein, Connors and Salinas, 1993). Schools are proud of their school-business partnerships, but not many students are involved in or benefited by these partnerships. Thus, one challenge of Type 6 activities is to assure greater equity in the access that students and families have to opportunities and experiences with business partners and other community services.

The framework of six types of involvement helps any school create a comprehensive program of partnership with families and with the community. There are hundreds of practices that can be selected to operationalize each type. As we noted, each type of involvement has serious challenges that get in the way of successfully reaching or involving all families. These problems must be solved through thoughtful program development activities.

Also, each type of involvement leads to different outcomes for students, families, and schools. Not all types lead quickly or directly to student achievement gains. One of the first results of each involvement type is parents' appreciation of the efforts by schools to keep them informed. When we first began studying practices of school-family partnerships in the early 1980s, we found that parents became involved who previously had not been involved, and parents immediately increased their regard and support for teachers. Another short-term result is that teachers change their attitudes about parents. As they increase their communications and interactions with parents, teachers begin to perceive parents as supporters. For example, at the start of one of the projects in a school in the League of Schools Reaching Out (Davies, 1990), teachers did not want volunteers in their classrooms. A project facilitator was successful in getting a few teachers to organize the work of volunteers and to use them well. During the course of the term, the facilitator received a succession of little notes from other teachers saying that they, too, were ready to accept a volunteer. It is important to recognize that teachers change their attitude as they watch partnership activities work.

The partnership process nurtures itself. Teachers become willing to communicate more with parents in different ways. Parents feel more welcome at the school and understand how to help at home. And, parent-child communications also increase.

There also are tangible results for students. Students whose teachers communicate frequently with their parents about learning activities at home do more homework than do other students, and have more positive attitudes about school, do more schoolwork on weekends, and benefit in specific skills (Epstein, 1991, 1992). Students at all grade levels and in all communities report that they want someone at home to talk with about school and homework. They are not so sure they want someone always at the school building. At the middle school level, however, children do not mind if parents or other volunteers are in classrooms assisting with enrichment programs. For example, middle schools students gave positive ratings to a program in which parent and other volunteers show and discuss art prints in their social studies classrooms, and learned something about art in the process (Epstein and Dauber, 1989).

Teachers take pride in sharing their progress and their problems, their observations and their plans with colleagues. We have been involved in programs with many inner-city elementary and middle schools for five years, and, more recently with a set of urban, suburban, and rural high schools. It has been extremely encouraging to observe the dynamics of teachers and parents sharing ideas, making plans, and improving their partnership.

Conclusion: Planning for Partnerships

To put the six types of involvement to work, educators must organize their work for action. This includes writing a policy of school and family partnerships that explicitly includes reference to goals for all of the types. Leadership is needed at the state, district, and school levels structure to guide program development, but ultimately, the work must be accomplished school by school. One way to assure that progress is made at the school level is to create an Action Team for School and Family Partnerships. With ideas from other teachers, parents, and students, the

Action Team (with an overall leader) is responsible for looking three years ahead to plan how the school will conduct its school, family, and community partnerships. The members of the Action Team become leaders of subcommittees for each of the types of involvement, adding or improving one or two practices for each type each year. Over three years, real progress can be made with practices to improve information to parents about child development, increase communication about school programs and student progress, increases and improves volunteers, designs better ways to encourage interactions at home about school work, increases parent participation in school decisions, and connects families and students to community resources and services. These are general goals for each of the six types of involvement.

This chapter illustrates an area of social science that has been energized and strengthened by a new theoretical view of social organizations that simultaneously influence children; by steady advances in research in sociology, psychology, anthropology, and education; and by a continuing collaboration of researchers and educators working together to help each other understand the possibilities and challenges of school, family, and community partnerships.

PART THREE

Family, School and Community Involvement: Special Population Issues

Introduction

Schools are finding it more and more difficult to educate all the children sent to them. While this is true generally, it is particularly so for those children with the fewest resources most in need of a good education. In the space of a scant quarter century the "Father Knows Best" family of the 1950s and 1960s has all but disappeared. In its place, single-parent families abound, mothers working outside the home are the norm rather than the exception, and many schools are so-called "majority minority" in which the majority of students are from minority or non-English speaking backgrounds. In addition, society appears to be less cohesive and more fragmented with many inner-city families suffering the greatest from poverty, crime and social dislocation. Schools are being asked to shoulder a greater and greater share of parental and community responsibilities and are finding their tasks more and more difficult. But, children spend 91 percent of their lives from birth through age 18 in places other than school, and parents—not professional educators—are children's most enduring teachers. If students are to be adequately educated, at a minimum, schools need parents, they need communities, and all three must work together and separately to serve the interest of the child, the student and the citizen. Often this means that teachers and principals must develop new understandings of the diverse families who entrust them to educate their children.

Following James Coleman's and Joyce Epstein's keynote presentations at the 1993 Milken Family Foundation National Education Conference a panel of educational researchers convened to discuss special issues associated with parent or family involvement in education. Addressed were issues concerning race or ethnicity, language minority families and socio-economic status and the schools.

Over the last quarter century research on school-family connections has progressed in two main directions. One strand of work focuses on the family and its characteristics, while the other strand focuses on the educational institution and its characteristics. The family-focused research suggests that patterns of family involvement in education are linked to specific family characteristics. For example, it has been found that parents of ethnically and linguistically diverse students as well as lower income parents do not participate in the schools in the same numbers as majority and higher income parents (Clark, 1983; Laosa, 1983; Comer, 1984; Delgado-Gaitan, 1990). The institutionally focused research on family-school connections suggests that school practices can and do affect parents' participation in their children's education. For example, Joyce Epstein's work has identified teacher "leaders" who successfully involve parents in their children's education regardless of family characteristics. Moreover, Epstein (Epstein and Dauber, 1989) found in a study of single and working parents that when teachers reached out to these parents, they were generally willing to become involved, and they can be as effective with their children as parents with more education and leisure.

Clearly, researchers agree that children have advantages when their parents support and encourage school activities (Clausen, 1966; Coleman et al., 1966; Mayeske, 1973; Heyns, 1978; Epstein and McPartland, 1979; Epstein, 1983); and that school and teachers can make the difference in parent participation (Delgado-Gaitan, 1991; Epstein, 1992). Indeed, students at all grade levels do better academically and have a more positive attitude toward school when their parents are aware, knowledgeable, and encouraging about school. Ann Henderson (1987, pp. 9-10), in her extensive review of the parental involvement literature, presents the following summary of what is known concerning parental/family involvement in children's education:

1. The family provides the primary educational environment.
2. Involving parents in their children's formal education improves student achievement.
3. Parent involvement is most effective when it is comprehensive, long lasting and well planned.
4. The benefits are not confined to early childhood or the elementary level; there are strong effects from involving parents continuously throughout high school.
5. Involving parents at home in their own child's education is not enough. To ensure the quality of schools as institutions serving the community, parents must be involved at all levels in the school.
6. Children from low income and minority families have the most to gain when schools involve parents. Parents do not have to be well educated to help.
7. We cannot look at the school and the home in isolation from one another; we must see how they interconnect with each other and with the community.

Yet even as researchers agree on these fundamental findings, shortcomings in parental involvement are widespread. Many researchers explain these shortcomings in terms of individual and societal circumstances. Specifically, it is suggested that family-school relationships are strongly affected by factors such as race, language and socioeconomic status. Furthermore, many believe that a family/school mismatch in these character- istics can significantly influence the quality and quantity of family-school interactions. In the chapters that follow, three well-regarded researchers discuss various aspects of family involvement in education under diverse educational and social and economic circumstances.

Socioeconomic Status and Parental Involvement in Schooling

In Chapter 4 Annette Lareau, a professor of sociology at Temple Uni- versity, discusses socioeconomic factors and their relationship to parental involvement in education. Lareau's (1989) research findings suggest that in spite of a shared positive value for education and a desire to see their children succeed, a disparity in parental involvement exists between middle- and upper middle-class parents and working-class or lower-class parents. Lareau notes:

- Not all families know how to become involved meaningfully in school-related activities.
- Not all schools and teachers know how to promote meaningful parental/family involvement for all parents and their children.
- Not all schools and families agree on the form and substance of parental involvement.

These circumstances, according to Dr. Lareau, are the predictable ac- companiment of social class membership. In a series of interviews, Lareau's research documented the family-school relationships in two el- ementary schools, one predominately white and working class the other predominately white and upper middle-class. At the 1993 Milken Na- tional Education Conference, Dr. Lareau reported on this research, dis- cussed her findings and made several policy recommendations.

The African American Family and the Schools

Dr. Diane Scott-Jones, a professor of psychology at Temple Univer- sity, approaches family-school involvement from the perspective of a de- velopmental psychologist as well as an African American parent who has seen a child through school. In her presentation, Scott-Jones stressed the unique experience of the African American family in dealing with the American public school system. She noted that historically it is an experience highlighted by mistrust and shaped by legal segregation and discrimination. In recent years African American families have had to contend with deficiency labels such a "culturally deprived" and "at-risk" students. Scott-Jones asserts that such terms are not useful in helping schools meet the needs of all students, but are rather nonsensical terms masquerading as scientific discourse. Such terms lower the self-esteem of students and tend to allow schools to shift the burden of educating students from the school to the home. Moreover, the growing racial discrepancy between the teachers and their students has intensified the difficulties in establishing supportive home-school relationships.

Having outlined some of the problems African American families face when dealing with schools, Scott-Jones asks an important question. Do schools want to involve families in a meaningful, respectful way in their children's education, or are they simply motivated to try to tell others how to be good parents? If the school's aim is, as it should be, to promote student success she makes several recommendations. First, barriers to family involvement, such as departmentalization that inhibits the development of close personal relationships between teachers and student, should be minimized. Second, educational jargon should be minimized in communication between teacher and parents. Third, teachers must believe that all children can and will succeed in school. Finally, she suggests that teacher training must do more to prepare teachers for the wide range of families they will encounter.

Such changes, according to Dr. Scott-Jones are often a matter of perspective. The change in perspective she suggests will not only help improve the relationship between African American families and schools but will help improve race relations in our country generally.

Involving Spanish-Speaking Families in Schools

The final speaker on the special topics panel was Dr. Concha Delgado-Gaitan. Dr. Delgado-Gaitan is a professor at the University of California, Davis and the author of *Literacy for Empowerment: The Role of Parents in Children's Education* (1990). The focus of Delgado-Gaitan's work is the dilemma faced by school and families when there is a language barrier between the home and the school. Essentially, regardless of good intentions on both sides, non-English speaking parents often are disenfranchised and cannot participate fully in their children's education. This disenfranchisement springs from the actions of both the English-speaking educators and the Spanish-speaking parents and often assures academic underachievement as the norm for Latino children.

Through an organization called COPLA and a process described as an "empowerment model," Delgado-Gaitan describes one Latino community's efforts to gain greater participation in their children's education.

Often schools communicate, and non-English speaking parents internalize, the message of parental deficiency. This message tends to be a self-fulfilling prophesy. Through the enabling process of critical reflection Latino parents shared their common history and experiences, identified their need for greater power, acquired knowledge, confronted stereotypes and constructed a system of support that ultimately led to greater meaningful communication between parents and teachers. In this way parents who had thought of themselves as lacking skills, who did not know the language of the schools—either spoken English or the formal language of education—empowered themselves and learned to help their children progress through school.

4

Parent Involvement in Schooling: A Dissenting View

Annette Lareau

It should be noted immediately that my comments in this chapter are critical of the notion of partnership so positively espoused in this volume. There is no doubt, in my view, that participating in family-school partnerships *can* be a valuable experience for children, parents and educators. But I find much of the policy debate to be overly simplistic, indeed, to be inaccurate and misconceived.

I maintain that scholars and educators have looked at the evidence regarding parent involvement selectively, concentrating almost exclusively on the *benefits* of such involvement. As a result, it is widely perceived among education commentators that parent involvement is an overwhelmingly positive good that should be embraced as broadly and as promptly as possible (Comer, 1980; Henderson, 1981; Epstein, 1987a; Rich, 1987; Coleman, this volume). My research suggests otherwise.[1]

There are three points I want to focus on: First, I believe there are implicit standards in teachers' requests for parent involvement. Many teachers want a limited form of parent involvement in schooling (Lorty, 1977); notably *positive* and *deferential* parent involvement; anger from and criticism by parents are looked upon less favorably. The standards teachers have in their minds for parent involvement are generally not well articulated in the literature.

Second, many teachers see parent involvement as reflecting parents' "concern" for education. The fact that parents' social resources affect their ability to comply with educators' standards is not widely recognized. Working-class and lower-class parents, who generally have only a high

Author's Note: I am grateful to Katherine Mooney, Evelyn Tribble and Leo Rigsby for their comments and criticisms on an earlier version of this paper. I remain responsible, of course, for the final product.

school education, often do not believe that they are knowledgeable enough to assist their children with school-related work (Lareau, 1989b). Parents who are college graduates rarely express such doubts. Similarly, the legacy of racial discrimination, for example, makes it more difficult for African American parents to be "positive" in their approach to school.

Compared to most white parents, many African American parents are much more suspicious about schools' agenda and more anxious about the possibility that their children will encounter institutional discrimination. Thus parents' social location by social class and race, rather than their relative level of concern, can make it more or less difficult for them to comply with teachers' requests.

Third, in addition to examining the implicit standards in educators' requests and the role of social resources in helping parents comply with teachers' requests, I want to discuss some of the social and psychological costs of parent involvement programs for children, parents, and educators. Parents' efforts to be involved in schooling, while well-intentioned, can discourage school achievement, disrupt family life, and create difficulties for teachers and principals.

These conclusions are drawn from a body of collected research using classroom observations undertaken intermittently over several years and across several geographical locations (Lareau, 1989a, 1989b, 1993).[2] During this period I also carried out two-hour, private interviews with mothers, fathers and guardians of the children I observed. Educational personnel, ranging from school secretaries to superintendents, were interviewed separately. This intensive qualitative research approach necessarily leads to quite small samples. The purpose, however, has not been to measure how common various parental or school practices are. Instead, my research has been, and continues to be, focused on identifying critical issues whose significance is frequently overlooked in our educational debates.

Implicit Standards of Teachers

Many educators are interested in parent involvement and express the opinion that they run their classrooms and schools using an open door policy. The type of parent involvement they typically have in mind, however, is quite limited in scope. As the superintendent of a small Midwestern elementary school district put it:

> I'd use words such as positive, encouraging, [and] supportive. Rather than being so defensive, trying to find out exactly what the circumstances were in the situation, trying to ask questions that zero in on what the problem is.

The importance of parents being "supportive" was also stressed by one of the third-grade teachers. When asked about the qualities of an ideal parent, she noted that:

> There are so many parents that automatically say that you are wrong and my child is right. The parents that I enjoyed working with the most were the ones who would listen to how the child is and what they needed to work on and didn't criticize you.

Teachers repeatedly praised parents who, in turn, had praised them. Teachers, as will be shown shortly, were less pleased when parents made criticisms, particularly those offered in a hostile and angry fashion. Most teachers were also interested in having parents defer to their professional expertise. Teachers appreciated parents who concurred with their assessment of a child, as this next comment makes clear:

> Jim Hughes' mother had a reasonable, rational, good understanding of her child's talents, strengths, and weaknesses. She did precisely what I said.

In their communications with parents, teachers frequently gave mixed messages. On the one hand, educators asked parents to be heavily involved in education. On the other hand, key aspects of schooling were defined by teachers as within their exclusive control. The implicit limitations on parents' control usually did not become explicit until conflicts arose. For example, educators rejected parents' suggestions that teachers be fired, that children be admitted to the gifted program even though they did not qualify, and that the curriculum be oriented less around work sheets.

Not only did teachers require that parent involvement be positive and deferential, but they minimized the teaching skills parents needed in order to be effectively involved in their children's schooling. Teachers often did not tell parents in advance how to handle common homework difficulties, such as basic reading problems involving stumbling over words in a book or challenging parents' answers as incorrect, but then criticized the actions the parents took when faced with these dilemmas. One working-class mother told a second-grade teacher in a parent-teacher conference that she forced her son to sound out words he could not readily pronounce on his own. The teacher dismissed that approach without discussion and instructed the mother to simply tell her son the proper pronunciation.

In downplaying their own considerable teaching skills, the teachers forgot that even allegedly simple tasks, such as selecting a book for a child, could be a complex undertaking for some parents. Consider this scenario, recounted by a first-grade teacher: A mother came to the school book fair to buy a book for her daughter Jill. At the end of first grade, Jill had the reading skills of a child entering first grade.

> She brought it to the room and asked if it would be all right for Jill. The book was at the end of second grade level or third; it was above Jill's abilities. I didn't want to hurt her feelings, but I remember telling her that Jill would feel more competent if she could start it. She really did not have her pinpointed in terms of her abilities. (Lareau, 1989b, p. 138)

Thus helping children with school work involved pedagogical skills parents often lacked. Although upper middle-class parents generally had more information about educational matters than working-class parents, even the upper middle-class parents were sometimes stumped by the work their children brought home from school. For example, one mother, who was a fourth-grade teacher, was bewildered by her third-grade daughter's math homework. She told her daughter, "Go see Daddy. Mommy doesn't do geometry."

Furthermore, there is considerable ambiguity about how much help parents should provide. By third grade, teachers expected children to show signs of responsibility regarding their own homework. They did not want the parent to take over responsibility for making sure it was completed. Parents' roles here were ambiguous: How much help would be considered too much help? Neither these areas of ambiguity nor the fact that some parents lack the skills necessary to help their children with schoolwork were commonly acknowledged.

Indeed, educators' discussions about parent involvement are exceedingly narrow regarding what constitutes involvement. Teachers often have in mind that parents will attend conferences, help with homework, volunteer in the classroom, and do fund raising for the school. Other contributions often go unrecognized. In some parents' eyes, simply getting their children up, dressed, fed and off to school in a timely fashion is a major contribution to their schooling. The disruptions to parents' schedules occasioned by early dismissals, snow days, and daytime-only parent-teacher conferences are generally ignored by school personnel.

To summarize, my first point is that schools have standards that are generally unarticulated but essentially focus on a narrow range of positive and supportive parental behaviors. Educators often miss actions that parents consider to be a legitimate part of their involvement in schooling. The narrow character of teachers' expectations and standards has not been considered in our policy discussions.

Social Resources and Parent Involvement

The existing standards for parent involvement in schooling are such that some parents are able to comply with teachers' expectations much more easily than other parents. For example, recent national surveys reveal considerable distrust on the part of African Americans of whites and white-dominated institutions. One survey (Jaynes and Williams, 1989, p. 134) found that 40 percent of African Americans believe that "on the whole most white people want to keep African Americans down." In a similar vein, only 7 percent of African Americans in another study reported that they feel they can trust most white people.[3] These and other measures of "African American alienation" from white society do not vary according to education and family income.

In addition, many of today's African American parents began their own schooling in segregated schools or in very recently integrated ones. Most of the African American grandparents of children in schools today experienced legalized racial segregation ranging from restrooms to employment.

This legacy of racial distrust has important consequences for parent involvement in schooling. Educators desire parents who are positive and supportive, but some African American parents approach schools with apprehension. One African American mother I interviewed, Mrs. Mason, felt that a "wave of prejudice" was sweeping the country and the community:

> It's the school system as a whole. Every now and then there is a wave of prejudice. It's almost like the law in America is now. You find a African American man that might commit a crime and he gets life for it and a white man might get off in a year and a half or he might get off with probation. So that's the state of law in America. That's a thing that we have to live with and we are living with it right now.

During the school year, Mrs. Mason objected to her daughter's placement in a reading group below grade level. She asked the teacher repeatedly to move the girl up. The teacher, who felt that the child's vocabulary was inadequate for a higher group, had her tested again, and then refused to change her reading group. Mrs. Mason also felt her daughter wasn't being called on enough during class. She was concerned about uneven distribution of punishment and felt that African American boys were being singled out for punishment.

Mrs. Mason shared her concerns with the teacher and the principal. Using an angry and confrontational style, she told the educators that they were treating African American children differently than white children. This expression of her concerns damaged her relationship with her child's teacher. The teacher resented Mrs. Mason's refusal to defer to her professional assessment of the child's reading skills, and she believed that the mother lacked a good understanding of her daughter's educational needs. She also felt that Mrs. Mason and her husband were too critical of everyone, including their daughter, with the result that the child was "insecure."

By the middle of the school year, the teacher, Mrs. Erickson, avoided interacting with the Masons. At the end of the year, Mrs. Erickson "boosted" the child's English grade a few points because, as she put it, "I just didn't want to have a scene." She found the Masons among the "most upsetting" parents in her teaching career; she was especially upset by their habit of raising their voices in conversation and "just out and out yelling."

Mr. and Mrs. Mason's very real interest and concern for their daughter's education was defined as intrusive and singularly unhelpful. The principal's assessment differed little from the teacher's. She saw only that the parents did "damage."

There is no question in my mind that the Masons were unusually angry and race-conscious compared with others in the school community. Their suspicions of racial discrimination, however, are widely shared by African Americans across the country (Jaynes and Williams, 1989). This legacy of racial discrimination means that, in general, it is more difficult for African American parents to approach the school in a positive and supportive fashion than for white parents. Because educators' standards call for parents not simply to be involved, but to be involved in a positive and supportive fashion, it is probably more difficult for African American parents than for white parents to build what teachers define as a successful relationship.

Parents' social class also influenced their skills and confidence in their ability to help their children educationally (Lareau, 1989b). Upper middle-class parents generally saw an interconnectedness between home and school and believed they had the right, and the responsibility, to supervise their children's schooling. As college graduates, most also had full confidence in their own ability to assist their children with school work. By contrast, working-class parents were likely to invoke a separation between home and school. They did not see themselves as integral to the educational process. One parent, who was a high school graduate, explained her role to me this way:

> I prepared them to go to school. That was my place. They had to learn, maybe, like you could say, basic structure. Behavior. You know, you don't throw things all over and you did what you were told, and things like

that. That was my job. And her job, [the teacher's] job, is to really teach them. She had gone to school to learn the best way to teach reading, mathematics, science, things like that. I don't know that. (Lareau, 1989b, p. 49)

Given what was usually a limited educational background, some working-class mothers preferred to turn over responsibility to teachers:

A teacher goes to school for a long time. They know a lot more than a regular person. I don't consider myself stupid, but I'm not extremely smart or intelligent. I could not go into a classroom and teach a class and expect them to come out knowing as much as the teacher teaches them. So I rely on the teacher's opinion a lot more than my own opinion. (p. 110)

Working-class parents expressed anxiety about their visits to schools; they could not always understand the teachers:

If they start using big words you think, "Oh God, what does that mean?" You know, it's just like going to the doctors. And it makes you feel a little insuperior to them. Because I don't have the education they do. You know, I just *don't*. (p. 108)

Thus even when their children were in primary grades, some parents did not feel capable of, and in some instances, did not appear to *be* capable of correctly helping their children with their schooling. Although disheartening, it is important to remember that an estimated 15 percent of adults are functionally illiterate (Venezky, Kaestle and Sum, 1987).

Thus my second point is that social resources, in this case race and social class position, may facilitate or impede parents' willingness and ability to comply with teachers' requests for their involvement in educational matters.

Costs

Third, although family-school partnerships are overwhelmingly defined as helpful for children, there is clear evidence that parents' actions can have unintended, negative consequences (Lareau, 1989b). In some schools, teachers routinely complained about parents acting in unhelpful ways that put too much pressure on their children. One principal noted that they were seeing more and more children with nervous problems, including stomach aches, bedwetting, and stealing. In some instances, the teachers linked children's behavior to their parents being involved in negative ways. The case of a first-grade low-achiever named Emily is instructive. During classroom observations, I noticed that Emily developed stomach aches, sometimes two or three times per week, during the reading period (Lareau, 1989b, pp. 149-150). Her mother was aware of the problem:

> It got to the point where she started at reading; during reading period she would get sick. Rose [the school secretary] would call me and say, "Well, Emily is in here again."

Emily also would not want to go to school, and she would cry when her mother quizzed her on words in the morning, before school:

> In January I put those words up on the refrigerator. She was coming home with words like "thrill" and "what" and "that." Every morning she would cry because she didn't know the words.

To make matters worse, her brother, a kindergartner, could and would read Emily's words:

> The thing was that Ross was knowing these words. He could damn well read all the lists of words.

In second grade, Emily's teacher was firmly convinced that this child's academic troubles were partially connected to the excessive pressure she endured at home:

> They put quite a bit a pressure on her, quite a bit of pressure. In terms of education and in terms of athletics. She swims every day.

The teacher also believed the parents constantly made invidious comparisons between Emily and her younger brother and that these comparisons "discouraged" Emily. Other teachers were also very worried about the excessive pressure parents placed on young children. They observed that overzealousness on parents' part created grave difficulties for some children.

Problems may extend to include parents' relationships with one another if they do not agree on how best to assist their children. One wife angrily recounted her husband's approach to helping their daughter:

> When she worked on flashcards, he would put her down. He would say, "Oh come on, Anna, you know these. You have seen these words before." Anna has a mechanism that when she feels pressure she freezes. When she freezes, Tom tries to force the answer out by pressure. And I know her, because she has my personality style, and that is the exactly opposite way to get the answer. (p. 155)

This woman felt strongly that her husband's behavior had a negative effect on their daughter's education, particularly on her motivation. Efforts to make the father change his tutoring style were unsuccessful.

Parent involvement in schooling is also potentially disruptive of family life if homework is allowed to become a battleground. One third-grade girl, Holly, regularly fought with her parents over schoolwork. Her father described the situation this way:

> Carol [her mother] has her for the first hour or so after she's home. She's real rough on Carol and won't do the work for her. I step in, and, you know, try to take over and get the two apart and see if we can start all over and get the work done.

Sometimes these conflicts spoiled the family's entire weekend:

> [Holly] stayed home the weekend to catch up on it [her homework]. Which, you know, she could have it very well done on Friday night and a little bit of Saturday, but she just will drag her feet and she just won't stay at it. You almost have to tie her in her chair. I tell her, I say look if it's gonna take you all weekend to do your work, you're gonna stay in there, and you're gonna do it, and you're not gonna get to ride the bike or do this or that. Whatever it takes. That's the way it's gonna be.

> Sunday morning came up, and [she] hadn't got it [done], and she said somethin' about goin' fishin'. So I told her, we will go all by ourselves, and we'll—you know she wanted to take the bicycles out—ride around the lake and fish and all that. I told her, I said if you get your homework done, then we'll go, but if you don't do the homework, you know, I'm not takin' ya to do these special things.

Her father estimated that, during that single weekend, there had been four or five occasions when Holly was crying and "real emotional" and three or four times when her mother was at the end of her rope. Finally, at 2:30 on Sunday afternoon, Holly finished her homework. Although these conflicts occurred regularly through the week and throughout the school year, Holly's parents never shared this information with her teacher. The substantial cost to family life that accompanied Holly's parents' involvement in her schooling went unacknowledged. Other families I interviewed reported similar battles in which parents lost their tempers and children stormed around the house.

The costs of parent involvement are borne by teachers, too. School and district programs to increase parent involvement frequently drained teachers' already limited time. For a single charity read-a-thon, for example, teachers needed to take time to tell the children about it, distribute the forms, collect the forms, remind children who forgot to bring in the forms, and promote the program in their classrooms by repeatedly reminding the children that the event was approaching. Classroom volunteer programs also created work for teachers, as they sought appropriate activities to assign to parents. Teachers, who had invested time and energy in developing lesson plans to include classroom volunteers, were understandably frustrated and resentful when these parents not only failed to show up but typically failed even to call to announce or explain their absence.

Communities with high levels of parent involvement in schooling frequently also had extensive informal information networks (Lareau, 1989b). Mothers talked with one another about what each had witnessed during their classroom visits. One principal I spoke with noted the destructive effect such information-sharing could have on teachers' morale:

> There is a rumor mill in this community that is really unbelievable. Teachers work *really* hard to have their job well done. Then to have parents come in and, in a sense, knife one of their peers in the back, by vicious verbal abuse that really depress[es] [the teachers] a whole lot. (pp. 162-163)

The undercurrent of criticism from parents in this community was ever present and surfaced at unexpected moments. One first-grade teacher, shopping in a store near her school, was subjected to an unsolicited monologue from the salesclerk regarding what he viewed as the poor quality of her colleagues' teaching skills. Thus, in communities with high levels of parent involvement in schooling, teachers may face increased emotional burdens as a result of being the object of criticism. They also may bear increased workloads as they struggle to meet parent and community concerns.

Principals, too, are affected by high levels of parent involvement. Interaction with parents, which one elementary school principal estimated took 20 percent of her time, decreased the amount of time principals had available for teachers, pupils, and school staff. Unrealistic demands on the part of parents could put principals in difficult positions. Few public school principals have the authority to fire teachers, yet unhappy parents expect that principals can and will resolve all problems in the classroom. Some parents exert tremendous pressure on principals, hoping to extract promises that their children will be assigned to classrooms with highly rated teachers.

Conclusion

To summarize, I have argued that we have had selective vision in the area of parent involvement in schooling. This selective vision has not taken sufficient account of the standards implicit within teachers' requests and the role of family background in facilitating parents' compliance with teachers' requests. Of course, policymakers may choose to accept the resulting costs as the necessary price for parent involvement. However, what they should *not* be allowed to do is continue simply to fail to calculate the negative consequences. Policy recommendations that do not consider the negative effects of parent involvement on children's self-esteem and motivation, on family dynamics, on teachers' leisure time, and on principals' job responsibilities are not merely short-sighted. The programs initiated are unlikely to succeed. It is essential that we collect more—and more accurate—information about *all* aspects of family-school partnerships. It is equally important that we actually use that full range of information as we design parent programs.

I would like to conclude with several policy recommendations. I fully believe that programs promoting parent involvement in schooling are of value. My suggestions, then, are not aimed at eliminating these programs, but at modifying them in recognition of the diverse character of peoples' lives.

Teachers are expected to convey to parents fairly complicated information in quite short periods of time. Teachers with a good reputation among parents often have excellent communication skills. School districts should devote substantial resources to improving *all* teachers' communication skills.

In addition, schools should look closely at the academic benefits associated with specific parent programs. Some, such as back to school night and open house night, require a very substantial amount of work on the teachers' part. They prepare work for their students, grade and post the work, and clean and decorate their classrooms. These events, including parent-teacher conferences, have become so highly ritualized that their academic benefits are minimal.

Educators might consider eliminating some events and taking steps to bolster the potential academic benefit of others, including parent-teacher conferences. For example, in preparing for their individual conversations with parents, teachers could draw up checklists of specific activities they would like parents to undertake. They could share some of their strategies for encouraging children to achieve their potential without subjecting them to excessive pressure. They could alert parents to watch for specific signs of tension in their children and suggest ways to increase unstructured time for play.

The role of social resources in shaping parents' compliance with teachers' standards must be recognized. Displays of anger by parents—even when grossly unfair to teachers—must not be allowed to destroy teacher-parent rapport. Conflicts between parents and teachers have a structural component. They are not likely to go away without large-scale changes in society at large. Because such changes will occur only slowly, if at all, we should develop programs aimed at broadening teachers' expectations to include more diverse parental styles. This does not mean displays of anger by parents are appropriate, desirable or fair. It does mean that educators should struggle for diverse strategies to sustain parent-teacher connections even in the face of conflict.

Regarding the uneasiness of some working-class and lower-class parents about their abilities to help their children with school work, I frankly think we should accept this self-appraisal. Parents who do not feel they have the ability to help should not be cajoled into doing so. These same parents, however, may be quite willing to arrange for an older sibling or cousin to help their children with school work.

Working-class and lower-class families often have extensive networks with family members within close proximity. These networks are an important resource that is not often tapped by school personnel. I would recommend that schools try to embed their efforts to recruit parent involvement within pre-existing social networks. Networks can be important tools for spreading informal information. For example, upper middle-class parents often have educators in their informal social networks. They turn to these friends and relatives for "inside information" about implicit school standards, including which rules are open to negotiation and which are not. Working-class and lower-class parents generally do not have similar access to educators. For them, disseminating information about school expectations through the media, including television, videos and radio, could be helpful.

Another approach would be to organize parent involvement programs through existing family groups. For example, read-a-thon competitions could challenge cousins to beat one another in the number of books read, and schools could facilitate a "buddy" system for homework where children would choose someone other than their parents, someone within their social world, to assist them with schooling. School officials need to deepen their knowledge of individual families' social networks and then tap into three or four points in these networks to build effective family-school interaction. Of course, this approach would entail more work for school personnel, as it does not presume a base at the classroom, school or even district level. Still, it is a potentially fruitful approach for certain populations.

Finally, despite these difficult economic times, schools should consider structural changes to facilitate parent-school contact. In most schools, it is very difficult for parents to get in touch with teachers during the work day. Many schools do not have a quiet space with telephones for teachers either to initiate or to return calls. Installing voice-mail systems would allow parents to leave teachers longer and more detailed messages about their concerns. Creating a private, quiet space where parents and teacher could meet at the school site would be useful. Purchasing adult-sized chairs for parents to sit in when they talk to teachers would increase both their physical comfort and their dignity. Finally, providing financial assistance to teachers for programs that they initiate to promote parent involvement could have an important impact.

Although I do not expect that I have been persuasive on all counts, my aim has been to provide evidence of the great disservice we do to families and children when we promote family-school partnership programs without explicitly acknowledging the considerable costs that may be involved. A better approach is to acknowledge the conflict these policies can generate and try to provide emotional and pedagogical tools for teachers, parents, and children to cope with this conflict. By thinking broadly about the different ways school-related expectations may be met, I believe we can increase some families' successful participation in their children's education. It is an important enterprise to many in the educational field.

Notes

1. This essay provides a reflection on the state of research on family-school partnerships. For a more systematic and critical assessment of the literature, see Lareau 1993.

2. My first research project is a study of family-school relationships in two first-grade classrooms (1989a). My most recent data, which I draw on below, is entitled "Managing Childhood, Social Class, and Race Differences in Parents' Management of Children's Organizational Lives: Excerpts from Field Study Interviews." This study of 16 white and 16 African American third-grade children is based on classroom observations and indepth interviews with mothers, fathers, guardians and professionals involved in these children's lives. Unless otherwise noted, all quotations below draw from this unpublished data set.

I am grateful to the Spencer Foundation, the National Science Foundation, Southern Illinois University and the American Sociological Association/National Science Foundation Small Grants Program.

3. Eighty-two percent reported they feel they can trust some white people and 11 percent reported they can trust no white people (Jaynes and Williams, 1989, p. 135).

5

African American Families and Schools: Toward Mutually Supportive Relationships

Diane Scott-Jones

All teachers and administrators have great opportunities for creating excellent schools, for influencing the development of our children, and through them, creating a better society. In this chapter I present my thoughts on African American families and schools.

Background and Goal

I have approached the issues involved in family, school and community partnerships in special populations from the perspective of a developmental psychologist. This is the area of study of human development across the life span, from conception through the end of life—from womb to tomb! As such, I am concerned with the processes that contribute to healthy development. I attempt here to identify the conditions that contribute to optimal development for all individuals. So I am concerned with the contexts of development and the interconnections among the contexts of development: families, communities and schools. This work is predicated on the belief that development is enhanced when the interconnections are strong among the contexts of development. Also, to understand development fully, we need to attend to historical and current social contexts of development.

I also write from the perspective of a parent who has raised one child and guided him through public schools. I have felt quite personally the joys and pleasures of rearing and educating a child, but I have also experienced the uncertainty parents inevitably feel as they attempt to meet the awesome responsibilities to their child. And I have also felt the particular difficulties of an African American parent raising an African American male child.

Finally, my views have been shaped by my own experiences as a student in public schools in a small southern town. Those schools were segregated then, and the students of my generation were responsible for integrating the high school in our town, and later, the universities in our state. In spite of the many problems, in spite of the denial of educational resources to those segregated schools, there was a wonderful interconnectedness of family, community and schools. A bond of trust existed among adults, and it encircled and nurtured children.

We cannot go back in time, however, to recapture that particular historical and social context of development. We would not want to, because there were many negative aspects of schooling at that time. Only a misguided nostalgia would cause us to return to a time when families, like my own, worked and were taxed to support schools their children could not attend. We can examine, however, how we can create in contemporary society mutually supportive families and schools, acting together to enhance children's education and development.

Let me emphasize *mutually supportive* families and schools. In discussing families, we must not shift the blame for students' poor performance from the school to the home. Instead, we hope that families and schools and all other institutions in society, including the healthcare system and the work place will act in concert to support children's development. Further, we must not impose our views on families or dictate to them how to raise their children. Instead, we seek partnership or collaboration with families.

Characteristics of African American Families

Historically, African Americans have made extraordinary efforts to maintain their families and to educate their children in the face of slavery, segregation and discrimination. African American families have a long history of working against obstacles. The historian, Herbert Gutman, in his book, *The Black Family in Slavery and Freedom*, has documented that African American families went to great lengths to stay in touch with one another and preserve family ties, even during slavery.

Similarly, educational historian, James D. Anderson, in his book, *The Education of Blacks in the South, 1860–1935*, shows the extraordinary efforts of African American families to educate their children. When public schools were first established, African American families were taxed, but the taxes were used to establish white-only schools. African Americans then raised the money for their own schools. So African

American families were *doubly* taxed for schools. African American families received help from philanthropists, such as Julius Rosenwald, but there was an enormous amount of self-help. One of the most poignant stories in Anderson's book is that of an elderly African American man, without any children of his own, who brought his life savings in a bag to a meeting to start a school in a small town in North Carolina. He had nothing to gain personally, because he had no children of his own; yet, he gave everything he had to start a school.

It is this historical picture of African American families and communities as strong and resilient that we must keep in mind. Even when they were denied opportunities to form families and denied opportunities to be educated, African American families made great efforts on their own behalf. This picture of African American families is in sharp contrast to that arising from social science research, which has focused on the presumed deficiencies of African American families. Much of social science research has contributed to negative stereotypes of African American families. Certainly African American families have problems, but these problems cannot be assumed to be essential or defining features of African American life and culture.

Presumed deficiencies are incorporated in the language we use to label people and problems. Demeaning phrases, such as "culturally deprived" have been used to describe African American families. As a teenager, when I heard or read the term "culturally deprived" used to describe African American families, I imagined that whites must spend their everyday lives engrossed in the art, the music, the literature, the culture of Western Europe. But when I first attended the formerly all-white high school in my hometown, I learned that white teens read *Mad* magazine and listened to James Brown and the Supremes! Then I thought that perhaps the culture African American families were deprived of had to do with etiquette and decorum and good manners. But when I went to the school cafeteria, instead of good table manners, I saw my first-ever food fight! As carefully as I looked, I couldn't find the evidence that African Americans were deprived of "culture" and that white Americans were filled with culture.

Later, as a student pursuing the study of psychology, I learned what "culturally deprived" really meant. It had little to do with the relatively superficial aspects of culture, such as popular music or how one eats or even what one eats. Instead, the phrase "culturally deprived" struck more deeply at what it means to be human. In one of the most influential research articles from the 1960s, it was said that the "meaning of deprivation is a deprivation of meaning" in the interaction between mothers and their children (Hess and Shipman, 1965, p. 885). This is a clever turn of phrase. Are we to believe that in low-income African American families, there is no meaning when a mother reprimands her child, there is no meaning when a mother expresses her affection for her child, there is no meaning when a mother teaches her child the everyday skills of living?

Of course, we now widely acknowledge that all racial groups have a culture and none could be said to be deprived of culture. But that phrase was widely used. The most influential text for teachers from the 1960s used in teacher training and in-service programs was titled *The Culturally Deprived Child*. Frank Reissman acknowledged that, although the term "culturally deprived" was inappropriate, he was using it because it was the popular, commonly accepted term (Banks, 1993). We must ask ourselves how a nonsensical term such as "culturally deprived" could gain scientific currency. Was it a mere convenience? Or do social scientists rush to embrace labels that encode the presumed deficiencies of ethnic minority groups?

In a recent book entitled *Playing in the Dark*, Toni Morrison, Pulitzer Prize winning author and Princeton professor, talks about dismissive language. Morrison says that white Americans use language to dismiss African American people, to establish them as "other." White Americans use language to create distance between themselves and groups they perceive to be different. Morrison's book is an eloquent but searing indictment of American race relations. Morrison asks whether white Americans have a powerful and insatiable need to assert racial and cultural superiority? After much criticism, the labels we use to describe African American families have changed. But new terms have been quickly substituted. The "at-risk" child is a term now commonly used. This term is unfortunate, for it locates difficulties *within* the child, and not in the environment external to the child. Families quickly learn the negative connotations of the new terms. A teacher described to me recently the reaction of an eighth-grade African American boy who was in a program for "at-risk" children. He asked why the teachers called them that name. He did not know what "at-risk" meant but he knew that it was nothing good.

We must forge a language for the discussion of race and culture. We cannot include nonsensical terms that masquerade as scientific discourse. Developing appropriate language will require much open discussion among people of different racial and ethnic groups.

Our difficult racial problems are exacerbated by the changing demographics of the student and teacher populations. Racial and ethnic minorities have increased in our society and increased in the student population (U.S. Bureau of Census, 1992). The racial composition of the teaching force, however, has moved in the opposite direction, with a higher proportion of white teachers and a lower proportion of African Americans and other minorities (National Center of Educational Statistics, 1992). The likelihood of difficulties in establishing home-school relationships is great, given the racial difference between the teaching force and the families they serve.

Another important issue for African American families is the pervasiveness of poverty. Of African American children, 44% live in poverty. This is only slightly higher than the rate for Hispanic children, which is 40%. Both these rates are higher than that for white children, which is 15% (U.S. Bureau of Census, 1992). Let me emphasize, however, that poverty is a problem for our whole society and not just for African American families. When we see a problem as limited to African American families, we tend to do less to remedy it. We tell ourselves that the problem is the result of deficient African American families. But 20% of all American children live in poverty (U.S. Bureau of Census, 1992). In the richest country in the world, one-fifth of all children are poor. We lead the industrialized world in the rate of childhood poverty (McFate, 1991). The U.S. rate is two to three times greater than that of most countries to which we are compared.

The United States fares most poorly on almost any measure related to the well-being of family. We have the highest rate of teenage childbearing of any industrialized country and a higher rate than that of some Third World countries (Jones et al., 1986). We have less available health care, less available day care—the list is long. These comparisons must cause us to question the strength of our national commitment to children and families.

When we look at all poor children in this country, however, the profile of poor children does not fit our stereotypes. Poverty rates are higher for African Americans and Hispanics than for whites; but the majority of children in this country are white, therefore, the majority of poor children are white. The majority of poor children do not live in the inner-cities, more than half live outside central cities. Much of poverty is in rural and suburban areas. And poverty is not limited to single parent families; more than one-third of all poor families are married couple families. The majority of poor families have at least one working parent, so the main reason families are poor is not that the adults refuse to work. Other problems assumed to be "African American problems" also exist more widely throughout society than we typically admit. For example, rates of teenage childbearing are higher for African Americans than for whites. But the majority of all teenage child-bearers are white (U.S. Bureau of Census, 1992). So, it is important to remember that problems that are great for the African American community are not limited to that community.

Developmental Needs of Children and Content of Programs

Any discussion of strong family involvement must begin with the legacy of Head Start. At its inception, Head Start included the notion of maximum feasible parent participation. The architects of Head Start believed that we should empower parents and involve them in the governance of Head Start programs. But somehow that notion of empowering parents was transformed as we proceeded to work on parent involvement in this country. We switched from empowering parents to trying to teach them how to be good parents (Hobbs, 1979). That is an important issue in involving families in schools. Do we want to involve families in a meaningful, respectful way, or are we simply motivated to try to tell others how to be good parents?

As a developmental psychologist, I am concerned with changes in the family's role from infancy through adolescence. What do parents do to help their children succeed in school? The answer to that question changes, as children grow and develop, and advance through the levels of school. What families do with preschool children and children in the early school years is very different from what is needed when those children become teenagers.

In the early years, learning is informal and children learn in their natural environments. The learning of language is a good example. Children learn their native language through their everyday social interactions with others. We do not sit down and drill young children on language day after day. Yet, all children learn their native language and they learn it well. Over time, this informal learning changes to the formal learning that is typical in schools. Through these changes children and families sometimes come to feel distant from the school. Entry into formal schooling is a critical transition point for children and their families. As children advance through the formal education system, their families may become less and less able to help them directly with their school work. This happens earlier for families with low educational levels than it does for parents with high educational levels.

In my work, I conceptualize three levels of parental influence: valuing, monitoring and helping (Scott-Jones, 1993). My work finds that almost all parents value education, almost all parents want their children to work hard and do well in school. So at this level, we find uniformity in parental values. At the next level, monitoring, we are concerned with what parents do to check their children's homework, to make sure that children are performing well in school. The monitoring extends to non-school behavior as well. Parents monitor where their children go and who their friends are. Parents monitor children's activities, such as television viewing, that might interfere with school work. The third level, helping, is where we find more difficulty.

We have two basic models of how helping can occur. One of these is the expert-novice model and the other is the model of learning together. In the expert-novice model, the parent is an expert helping a child who is less skilled. In the second model, learning together, both parent and child are learning the topic at the same time. To illustrate the difficulties that arise as parents try to maintain the expert-novice model, I can use myself as an example. When my son was in eighth grade, he asked for help with a difficult algebra problem. Of course, I did my very best to help him, but it took me 20 minutes to work the problem. I had to look in the back of the book to make sure the answer was correct. I was very proud of myself. But my son, without ever informing me of his decision, after that day always asked my husband for help with math homework; he has an undergraduate degree in mathematics. I helped my son with other school subjects for which I was a better "expert." The point is that many families lose their ability to be experts much earlier than I did. For some parents, this occurs as early as third or fourth grade. In a study I conducted of first-graders and their families, some parents were lacking in the skills—for example, in reading and spelling—they were trying to teach their children (Scott-Jones, 1987).

Children, as they progress through school, close the knowledge gap between themselves and their parents. So, many parents are not able to help directly with homework anymore. But they can contribute immeasurably to their children's education in other ways, by monitoring their children's school performance and other activities and by continuing to convey to their children that education is highly valued.

Another aspect of family life that changes as children move through the school years is the relationship between the parent and child. When children are very young, they value close relationships with parents. As children get older, they are more and more involved with their peers and with others who are outside the family. So, the close involvement of a parent and child may change, especially during adolescence, and this may interfere with parents' being able to help children with school work in a positive manner. In thinking about parental involvement, we must keep in mind that the foremost job of parents is to provide acceptance and love for their children. The responsiveness of parents to their children is an important part of parent-child relationships. We must not lose sight of the acceptance and love that characterize healthy parent-child relationships. We use the metaphors of schooling, such as "curriculum of the home" to describe what families do. But a home is not a school and parents are more than teachers in their relationships with their children. We use the term "responsiveness" to describe this aspect of a parent's involvement with their child. Parents need to be responsive and warm and loving with their child in addition to making sure that they do well in school.

Family Involvement at School

Family involvement in activities at school is important. One of the most comprehensive programs for African American families was developed by James Comer (1980). In establishing his programs, he found that parent involvement waxed and waned over the years, and tended to be crisis-oriented. Parents tended to be more involved when something had happened to draw their attention to the schools. Comer found that parents—50-100%—were involved in fund raisers, social events, and conferences with teachers. At the next level of involvement, 10-25% of parents were involved in tutoring in classrooms, assisting with field trips, and the like. At the most influential level of parental involvement, only 1-5% of parents were involved in decision making regarding curriculum, personnel and governance of the school.

Schools, however, can become centers of family and community activity. Families and communities should feel a sense of belonging and a sense of ownership of schools. At one urban high school where we work, the principal sees his school as a "lighthouse" for the community. A vast array of programs and activities for families and communities are provided in the school building. This welcoming of families and communities is necessary in order for parents to move toward more active involvement in the classrooms and in school governance.

There are some barriers to family-school connections in our school system. First of all, the structure of schools can be an impediment, particularly in middle schools and high schools. Once teaching becomes departmentalized and a child has many teachers, maintaining personal relationships among parents, teachers, and students becomes more difficult.

The nature of communication between school and home is important. Often the communications parents receive from school are filled with educational jargon. Families without high educational levels may feel unable to communicate with teachers in the language they use.

A final barrier is belief about families and children. It is important to believe that all children are capable of learning and that all families have worth and value. Unless those beliefs are present and strong, involving families in school activities will be difficult.

Teacher training, unfortunately, typically does not focus on family involvement. Teachers receive very little preparation for the wide range of families they will encounter. The little discussion of families in teacher preparation programs is likely to be negative. Teacher training should focus on positive as well as negative aspects of families. Currently, most teachers learn on their own about how to involve families in their activities.

Looking Toward the Future

When we institute family involvement programs, it is important to assess their success. How do we define success in programs to involve African American families in schools? Usually, the gains are small and progress is slow. In evaluating parent involvement efforts, we must be concerned about process—how we implement programs; as well as outcomes—how many parents became involved or how much their students improve. Further, we must acknowledge that broad comprehensive programs and policies, geared to characteristics of children, families, and schools, are needed in addition to our relatively small-scale efforts. So, even when gains are small and progress slow, we must maintain our commitment to involvement in schools as a right and responsibility of families.

I want to reiterate my concern regarding race relations in this country. It seems that race relations have deteriorated rather than improved over the past couple of decades. We must find ways to work together to meet our common goals. And we must acknowledge that we need each other to meet those goals. I have faith that we as a society can do these things.

When I think about my goals for race relations in this country, I think often of my favorite childhood toy, which was a kaleidoscope. As a child I was fascinated by the fact that with just a small twist, the multi-colored pieces in the kaleidoscope would fall together in ever-more beautiful patterns. And I think that about our race relations. With just a small shift in our perspective, we can come together in ways that would create a more beautifully patterned society.

6

Spanish-Speaking Families' Involvement in Schools

Concha Delgado-Gaitan

Family-school interaction has, for a long time, been the focus of my research. Indeed, for the past 10 years, family, school and community relationships have been at the heart of my research agenda, but not solely as an academic exercise.

As an elementary school teacher, I met my students two weeks before school opened at their homes. I visited every one of them, individually, met their families, and got to know them. I believe that this out-of-school contact created a very strong connection that continued into the classroom. Later, as the school principal, I made our school a "community school." This meant that the school was open to our entire community—in whatever way we could have them participate—so that any group would have use of the building. This helped to make the school an integral part of the community. My research work in Carpinteria, California has offered me a setting where boundaries between researcher, educator and family have been blurred in an effort to build holistic learning environments for Spanish-speaking Latino children.

Carpinteria: A Case Study

As a basis for my discussion here, I review my experience in Carpinteria. A rural and resort community about 20 miles south of Santa Barbara in Southern California, it has a population of approximately 12,000. For a long time, the city was segregated—the Latino community was isolated socially, economically, linguistically and geographically. Latinos comprise 45% of the population and most are Spanish-speaking. Latino students in Carpinteria went to segregated schools until the early 1970s when federal programs were solicited by the school district to provide compensatory education to Latino students.

In spite of efforts undertaken by individuals in the school district to ameliorate the academic under-achievement of Latino students, academic under-achievement was the norm within the isolated Latino community and Latinos had no voice in the schools. Part of my research work in Carpinteria was to *build on* community strength so that this community became more actively involved, on a broader social level, within the school as well as with the outside community. Latino families empowered themselves through an organization they named COPLA, *Comite de Padres Latinos* (Committee for Latino Parents).

Latino parents organized and mobilized to accomplish three major goals: (1) to support each other as families with a common culture and language, (2) to cooperate with the schools in order to learn better methods for assisting in their children's schooling, and (3) collectively to engineer the school's direction to improve educational outcomes of Latino students.

The process that most characterized the mobilization and the development of COPLA can be described as an "empowerment model." COPLA parents built on their strengths—their common history and experience in Mexico and Carpinteria. They shared concerns, troubles and potential with each other. By engaging in this type of critical reflection, they broke some cultural stereotypes that others recognized as limiting and therefore were able to explore ways to work with the school and with their families. What began as a district-wide committee of 12 people has now organized a local COPLA committee in all of the Carpinteria schools: 3 elementary, 1 middle school and 1 high school. Each local committee deals with the needs of Latino children in the respective schools.

The Beginnings

Despite attempts by federal programs to manage and correct academic underachievement, Latino parents perceived the need for greater and different efforts. The initial planning group of COPLA recognized that some parents were more skillful than others in ways to help their children in school. COPLA drew on the expertise of these members to train and aid the less skillful in its group. This process of mobilization increased parental "awareness," a critical element in motivating parental involvement.

Awareness, in the context of parent education, refers to the consciousness of these Spanish-speaking parents about their role in the social environment and the conditions under which they could operate most efficiently as fundamental agents for change (Delgado-Gaitan, 1991). COPLA's initial small parent nucleus met and shared experiences; they identified what they saw as the Latino community's need for training in ways to communicate with school as well as strategies to help their children with homework. These parents also recognized that there was a general lack of information in their community regarding schools. They committed themselves to learning how schools operate and how parents could participate most effectively.

The process of empowerment was an intentional process centered in the local community. Key to its development was mutual respect, critical reflection, caring and group participation. These tenets allowed a group of people who lacked an equal share of valued resources the ability to gain greater access to and control over those resources.

Implicit in the process of empowerment undertaken by COPLA was a consciousness of as well as a responsibility for individual member's behavior. COPLA members made clear their willingness to take action to shape the schools and their children's education—as they desired—through a social process which I will describe below.[1]

Empowerment: The Core

Central to the ability of the COPLA group to become empowered was the concept of a "critical reflection process." I have defined this elsewhere as:

> a process that engages people in careful examination of the assumptions that guide self, family, and institutional norms, values, policies, and decisions that direct our lives including institutional policies and practices in government, education, and other social services. As a consequence, the group's awareness of their shared experience (past and present) becomes the basis for collective action (Delgado-Gaitan, 1991, p. 34).

The major assumptions of this critical reflection process were observed in the formation of COPLA. They are outlined as follows:

1. Parents discuss their common history and experience with schools.
2. Parents share their realization that their feelings of isolation in the community are common to most parents, yet specific to Spanish-speaking families because of a lack of power and representation.
3. Parents acknowledge that there exists a lack of information regarding schools and commit themselves to learning how schools operate and how parents can participate most effectively.
4. Parents confront common stereotypes imposed on them that create limitations in their school involvement. For example, they dispel the notions that their limited English ability prevents involvement

with the school, that their limited formal education prohibits their involvement, that working long hours excuses their participation, and that Latinos cannot organize themselves.

5. Parents construct an egalitarian system of interaction to relate to each other during their meetings based on mutual respect for everyone's ideas.

6. Parents realize that maximum support for their children's education means mutual cooperation between families and schools.

7. Parents resolve to organize activities designed to encourage frequent and meaningful interaction between parents and teachers. (Delgado-Gaitan, 1991, pp. 34-35)

Models of School-Family Interactions

To understand the means of empowerment undertaken by COPLA, we need to put families and school relationships into a workable framework. The power relations schema shown in Figure 6.1 illustrates the different levels of shared power and its possibilities.

Conventional parent involvement activities are one-dimensional relationships. This type of activity uses open house and teacher conferences as the principal avenues to communicate with parents. The one-dimensional type of interaction is one in which the school dictates and defines

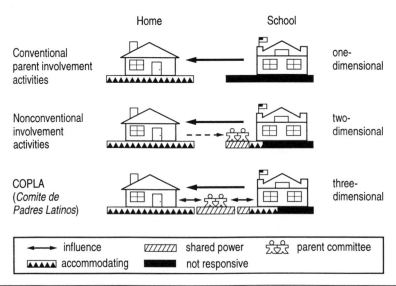

FIGURE 6.1

the avenues whereby families participate in the schools. Generally, parents do not have a problem getting to these traditional events, but the nature of the experience limits the kinds of contact that parents and schools have. Some teachers continue to feel that this is what they *want* to define as family contact. And, yet, some of these educators also continue to complain that Latino parents do not participate in their children's education. We found that the open house forum and parent-teacher conferences provide minimal opportunity for information exchange.

In the nonconventional involvement activities shown in Figure 6.1, a two-dimensional model exists. This includes special avenues that are opened as a result of mandated federal projects, such as migrant education, preschool education, and bilingual education.

In a two-dimensional type of interaction, schools and families connect, such as in preschool programs or Head Start. Here, government program guidelines spell out "parent involvement." This explicit program imperative results in more meetings of parents and educators. Spanish-speaking parents become involved in larger numbers. For the most part, however, the environment remains one in which the school is the authority and continues to teach parents about the ideas, activities, and goals the school believes families should know. The presumption is that parents are generally unaware of certain issues, such as AIDS, immigration rights, grades, or larger, more critical problems at the school. In this model, relations between home and school are expanded and more interaction occurs.

There are times when this form of parent involvement is a critical first step toward the reduction of isolation: Parents are made aware that an interest group of like people exists and possible connections with others in their communities are presented. It was during this phase in Carpinteria that the building blocks of COPLA were formed.

In a three-dimensional model, as shown in Figure 6.1, these types of relations are exemplified by the organization of COPLA. Decisions on what families need to learn and how they want to communicate with the school are addressed in organizational meetings. This model is defined by the organization in cooperation with the school. In the three-dimensional model, a power relation exists where parents decide they need to come together, to organize and negotiate with schools to develop supportive learning environments for students both at home and school.

The Language Dilemma

In Carpinteria the school believed and communicated a notion of deficiency to the parents, that is, parents did not have the language necessary to communicate with the teachers. By "language" they meant not only English, but the language used in school communications and the language used to provide homework guidance. My research showed that teachers firmly believed that Latino children did not have the appropriate support at home (Delgado-Gaitan, 1992). As a result, these children were not placed in advanced groups but were relegated to more novice learning settings.

Parents internalized these school-held beliefs and sought to understand why it was their families were not communicating at a level necessary—as they perceived it—to hold the family together. This fundamental issue made itself known through critical reflection processes undertaken, in part, in COPLA meetings. Children were learning more English than the parents could, but parents were dissatisfied with what the children were learning at school. Carpinteria parents felt discouraged because in spite of great sacrifices made to immigrate to the United States, their children underachieved. These parents were concerned that something in their home was missing. And so, they sought ways to fortify their home.

During this process of reflection parents began to trust each other. They came to understand that they were not alone, that they had the ability to communicate with each other, with their children, and with the schools. And these shared experiences—prior to relocating to the United States and after their arrival here—informed their lives and directed their relationships with their children. They conceded that although they did not have formal schooling in the United States, they had the knowledge, information and experience to communicate with their children. Indeed, sharing their world view was necessary and important to the communication with their children. It was in the language of the home that this communication would occur even though many were taking English as a second language classes. COPLA conducted critically important work to dispel the school's poorly founded notions of parental deficiency.

Levels of Parent Participation in Children's Education

Contrary to the school's beliefs that Spanish-speaking parents did not or could not work with children in partnership with school, parents did assist their children in numerous ways prior to COPLA. My study showed that home activities related to school work were complex and suggest genuine caring and support on the part of adults in the home.

Parents varied in the way they worked with their children in Carpinteria. The parent's knowledge about the subject matter and their available time factored into the nature of their home literacy activity with their children.

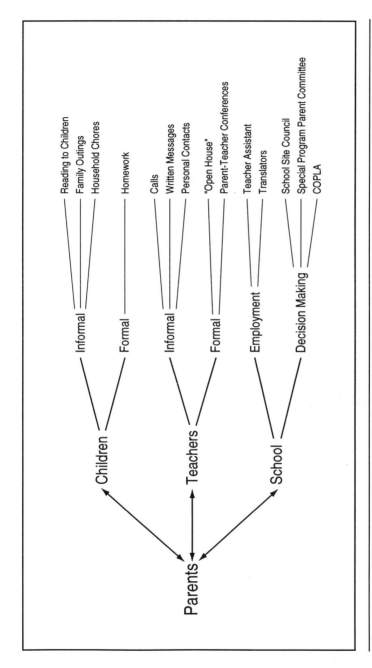

FIGURE 6.2 Levels of Parent Participation in Children's Education

Home Activities Related to School Work

After the formation of COPLA, the organization studied the home life of Carpinteria students. It confirmed that rich communication existed in the home and intricate activities occurred involving written and oral text. For example, parents interacted with their children around homework. They discussed completed homework, engaged in oral literacy by reading their children's favorite storybooks, motivated children to read independently, discussed school reports with children, engaged children with personal literacy materials (e.g., letters), and parents studied English as a second language.

Regardless of the fact that parents and caretakers communicated with children about schooling, Latino parents continued to be isolated: Many simply did not know how to deal with the school. COPLA transformed this situation.

Bilingual Program: A Step Toward Change

COPLA parents collectively decided to pursue complaints regarding school policy and teaching methods in an organized manner. One of their first efforts involved the review of the bilingual program. Parents believed the bilingual program underserved their children: Latino students performed poorly in school even with the intervention of a bilingual program. The grievance process included numerous meetings with the schools. Educational issues are rarely resolved in one meeting. The

1. Parent/child homework activity

2. Parents oral literacy related talk

3. Parents reading with children

4. Parents motivating children to read

5. Parents discuss completed homework

6. Parents discuss school reports with children

7. Personal literacy materials (letters, etc.)

8. Parents study English as a second language

FIGURE 6.3 Home Activities Related to Text

strength of the COPLA empowerment process was that it worked in a series of face-to-face dialogues between families and educators. The process was based on honesty and a commitment to cooperation. As a result, COPLA was empowered, though the changes they sought occurred gradually (see Figure 6.4).

The results of the COPLA organization were recognized immediately as Latino parents organized themselves. Latino parents shared with each other those practices that helped their children in the home. They also assisted each other in communicating with school personnel. The support that parents exchanged increased their access to the schools and allowed them to help their children more effectively.

COPLA was not a limited intervention. It evolved and expanded as parents developed their skills in communicating with the schools. In the three-dimensional model represented by COPLA, parents agree to make necessary changes, both in the home and in their communication with the schools, that will promote the overall education of their children. The agendas are theirs and they, along with the schools, determine how they will proceed to make those changes. The joint effort on the part of schools and the parents enables both the family and the schools to benefit. When both institutions cooperate, problems are solved more readily. The empowerment process provides a context for discourse which makes negotiation possible. Basic premises underlying the process assume that people affected by specific services, in this case, the families affected by the school

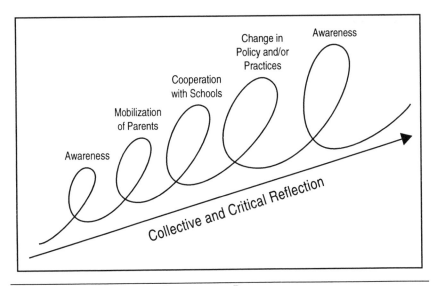

FIGURE 6.4 Parent Involvement Empowerment Process

programs, are the most capable of making choices and decisions toward resolution of conflicts. It is important to note that local COPLA meetings involve both teachers and parents. They define areas with which teachers should be familiar to work more effectively with Latino students.

Parents as Teacher Advocates and Teachers as Advocates of Latino Families

Parents became strong teacher advocates through participation in COPLA. They learned to recognize that teachers try to help their children the best way they can. Parent's also recognized that teachers' jobs can be rendered more effectively when they have the support of parents.

Teachers *need* to be advocates of Latino families: This is a basic premise of the COPLA program. Teachers must first acknowledge that Latino parents care about their children's education and they want that education to be a good one. If parents are not involved to the extent the teacher or school wants them to be, it is because they do not know how the school works and feel incompetent to communicate with the school. These parents may also have negative experiences where the school has made them feel powerless.

Further, teachers need to appreciate that when parents participate in their children's schooling, academic performance improves. Thus, teachers need to engage parents in multiple and diverse ways to enhance academic performance. For this to happen, parents must be involved as an integral part of the curriculum. That means teachers must make parents their co-teachers so that when the school goes home, parents stand a better chance of reinforcing what is learned in the classroom.

Communication—frequent and understandable—between teachers and parents must be established through a variety of means. Some examples follow.

Information must be shared which can enhance students' learning opportunities. This communication should not concentrate solely on negative reports. Teachers are obligated to utilize students' home culture as part of the classroom curriculum to make students' language, culture and history a part of the daily program. Finally, teachers need to remember that student differences do not make them deficient.

In Carpinteria, parents who thought of themselves as not having skills, who did not know the language of the schools—either spoken English or the formal language of education—empowered themselves through COPLA. They came to view this empowerment not just as a right but also a responsibility. They recognized the urgency to organize and assume responsibility for a range of activities between home and school. And it is in the mobilization of parents by other parents that knowledge is transferred in a way that is significant: Formal education is not required for parents to hold leadership positions in the community.

Carpinteria parents and educators pursued a common purpose through COPLA's efforts. As a result, a shift occurred in the practices and policies of the schools. Another key shift occurred as parents recognized that even as it was necessary for the children to learn English, and for the teachers to have appropriate materials and adequate programs to teach their children, the parents themselves needed to take an active role in the process. In recognition of their need to be partners in their children's education, many of these parents participated in English as a Second Language program as a result of the amnesty mandate. Now they took on more classes and became more involved in their own education. They used their family practices as a way to model their understanding of how necessary education is and how important English is to that education.

Specifically, the success of COPLA can be measured by the academic progress that Latino children made once parents were able to obtain special tutoring for underachieving children. As a result of increased teacher and parent interaction students advanced in their literacy placement. About 99% of parents with children in first through sixth grade who attended regular COPLA meetings reported that their children's literacy grades improved at least one full grade within one report period. Teachers reported increased communication with parents who initiated meetings to learn how to help their children at home. Teachers also noted that Latino parents asked more informed questions about their children's progress and the classroom curriculum, which held teachers more accountable. A case example involved Mrs. Juarez and her fifth-grade daughter, Berta, who was having difficulty both emotionally and academically. Mrs. Juarez attended COPLA meetings regularly. Rather than blaming her daughter for not liking school, she learned how to contact the teacher and ask about Berta's learning problems. The teacher commented that the mother's increased interest seemed to have improved Berta's confidence in the classroom as she became more enthusiastic about her success. Berta commented, "I can't read as fast as other kids but I'm trying harder now and I think I'll make it to sixth grade and I feel good about that."

Conclusion

In my book, *Literacy for Empowerment*, I stated, "A key goal of the COPLA organization has been for parents to learn from each other ways to help their children progress through school and to become a support system for each other" (Delgado-Gaitan, 1991, p. 33). Based on my experiences with COPLA and a wide range of studies I have pursued involving Latino family-school interaction, it is my opinion that where sociocultural congruency exists between home and school settings, children have a greater chance of succeeding in school. Parents who are knowledgeable about the school's expectations and the way in which the school operates are better advocates for their children than parents who lack such skills (Delgado-Gaitan, 1991).

What has taken place through the development of COPLA in Carpinteria, California, is a small example of the potential for positive change in Latino student achievement and Latino family participation in schools. COPLA recognizes and utilizes individuals' strengths in the face of the perceived deficits. COPLA accepts that parents participate in their children's education in a socially and culturally defined process.

Individuals are empowered when they involve themselves directly in the process for change. When allowed to build on their strengths, families win; they validate their day-to-day experience in communicating with their children. Educators also win because families communicate more frequently with school. And, children win because they feel supported by adults in both their household and school settings.

Ultimately, through on-going dialogue, the power relationship between Latino families, schools and communities can become more balanced as the focus shifts from school-only decision making to school-family decision making that makes children of central importance.

It is realistic to establish structural means that support school efforts for involving parents in their children's education beyond a superficial level. Key elements of the kind of structural support needed are: (a) Teachers need release time to meet with parents when it is convenient for both; (b) Principals need adequate funding to hire personnel who speak the language of the major language groups in the community; (c) Schools must invest in a complete parent education program, from preschool to high school. COPLA formed in an elementary school setting but its usefulness continues throughout the school years.

Only with a total commitment of policies and funding, and well-developed plans from the state, county, district, and the local school, may educators expect those who have little comprehension of the school system to be active in the schools. COPLA provided a framework that has sparked new cooperation and understanding between Latino families and schools, greatly enhancing the education and well-being of children, parents and teachers alike.

Note

1. This composite definition of Latino empowerment includes elements taken from works by Allen et al., 1989; Delgado-Gaitan, 1990; and Freire, 1970.

School-Parent Partnerships in Minority-Based Communities: A Program for Positive Interaction

Introduction

In Part Four this volume focuses on implementation issues involved in family, community and school interaction. What are the nuts and bolts of family and community involvement programs at the district and school levels? How do teachers and administrators make these relationships work in the classroom? What are the steps that make a program successful day in and day out? In these chapters, two highly innovative practitioners present their ideas on implementation in minority-based communities. Authors Perez and Daher present well-developed, extensively tested programs that have been implemented in Texas, California and Washington state.

Partnership Potential

In chapter seven, Pablo Perez discusses his nationally recognized program in McAllen, Texas. Perez is a long-time activist in the area of family, community and school interactions; a former teacher and principal in Texas, Perez was superintendent of the McAllen School District until he joined the Pasco, Washington, School District No. 1 as superintendent. The McAllen, Texas, schools have a large Mexican population and a substantial Chapter 1 program. It has been estimated by the McAllen district staff that nearly 99% of parents had some productive contact with their children's school under Perez's leadership. When his students began migrating in significant numbers to Pasco, Dr. Perez moved to Washington to implement his program there. In this chapter, he outlines how the program functions in Pasco, a place Perez calls "a little United Nations."

Perez's program—tested over a period of years—requires a base-line commitment on the part of educators to the idea that all students *can* learn. But more than that: Dr. Perez demands educators look to themselves to discern what it is that they are doing to keep the education process from being a success. Perez's ideas require educators to involve themselves broadly in the education of their students, reaching from classroom to school to home and back to school in a program designed to meet the needs of the extended minority family.

Perez's ideas are both practical and pragmatic. He believes that the static classroom educator must give way to educators who are actively involved in their community's needs. Educators are called upon to create "user-friendly schools," linguistically and culturally friendly to the changed cultural configuration represented by students—requiring both flexibility and well-developed communication skills from educators. In Perez's program, positive leadership and powerful motivation are critical to the successful interaction of families and schools.

Partnerships: A Guide

The final speaker at the National Education Conference, session on implementation issues, was Judy Daher. Daher is deputy superintendent of the Redwood City School District in Northern California and has a fully operational, extensively tested program of school-family partnerships working throughout the Redwood City School District.

The program she advocates and the strategies she discusses require system-wide efforts. It is a program of participation and cooperation at all levels: district, administration, school site and family. For the program to work participants must agree to systemic change and a long-term time commitment of three to five years.

The first step, according to Daher, is planning: Teachers and administrators need to delineate objectives for family involvement with "recognizable milestones"; clearly defined methods for regular community input and feedback are required; and family involvement must be established as a priority. Productive interaction can be implemented at all levels once these prerequisites are met. Daher outlines an entire program of interaction that is operational in Redwood.

Daher's program need not be a hierarchical process and can be implemented through family and educator collaboration. She outlines numerous examples of positive structural changes—none require contractual modifications and, she asserts, all are "relatively easy to implement" (p. 114). The most basic of the structural changes is the formulation of a district-wide (and then school-site) mission statement that provides the basis for a parent-community-school partnership plan.

On-site adminstrative staff, parents or significant adults as well as educators are all key players in the effective functioning of the Daher program. Daher's plan involves the successful integration of the efforts and effects of structure, staff and parents/significant adults. Recognizing that human behavior is difficult to change and that the process takes place over a period of time, her program offers numerous examples of on-site activities that have proven successful. Daher calls upon knowledge of families, effective communication and time management for all participants in this process. More than any other chapter in this volume, Daher's program offers practitioners a guide to school-family-community interaction.

7

Partnership Potential:
The Importance of Working
Toward Positive Outcomes

Pablo Perez

McAllen, Texas to Pasco, Washington: An Ongoing Exchange

A couple of years ago I learned that some of the youngsters from my district in McAllen, Texas, were migrating to southeastern Washington state. I visited Pasco, Washington, and decided to coordinate district efforts in that particular part of the country. We were able to establish an exchange program of teachers and principals so that we could make school better for children as they migrated back and forth between Washington and Texas.

I call Pasco the "Little United Nations." The majority of children are minority students (about 52%): Hispanics, Latinos, Asians, African Americans, a tremendous rush of new students in large numbers. Pasco offered a wonderful opportunity for us to make things work for these children. It offered a tremendous opportunity to make things work the way they should work in a country that represents all groups. The Pasco District has 7500 children that are eager and ready to learn. But these students have an added challenge in a district with so many different ethnic and minority groups. We, as educators, needed to acknowledge, work with, understand, respect and bring together all of the different cultures represented in Pasco.

Practitioner's Outlook

I start with the idea that practitioners want parents to participate. And, if educators are to be successful at parental participation, we need to set our "house" in order. Educators must ask themselves, "What is it that we have within our institution that's keeping people away?" Certainly, it is not that parents do not want to participate. And, certainly, it is not that they are not interested. Educators need to take a look at ourselves, clean up what parents may see as negative and move forward. Second, I address some of the practices—I cannot mention them all—that were developed in McAllen and are now used in Pasco. I discuss implementation and what the success has been.

If educators want parents to know that they are interested in parental participation, educators must talk about how they *feel* about children. If *teachers* do not believe that all children can learn, then educators are sending the wrong message. It is essential that teachers let parents know that regardless of who parents are and where their children came from, whether they speak English, Spanish or other languages, that all children *will be successful.* If educators tell that to parents, they will be ready to come in and do some work.

User-Friendly Schools

Voicing these positive beliefs is one thing—because that is the talk— but "walking the talk" is a different thing. Teachers and administrators must ask themselves, "What is it in my institution that is turning kids off?" If students are turned off in school, the correlation will be direct: Parents will also be turned off.

If students represent a different configuration in the cultural framework than educators do, then we need to have an institution that is not only linguistically friendly but culturally friendly to these children as well. By way of example, a first-grader comes in anxious to learn. The child has been told that school is the best thing since sliced bread or round tortillas. This child is *eager* to learn. He hits that first-grade classroom ready to go, except his name is Pablo and he knows no English. He sits down and this wonderful first-grade teacher talks to Pablo in a language he does not understand. He says to himself, "What am I going to do now?" He is so happy to be in school and, by his second day, he has fallen in love with the first-grade teacher. The teacher begins the unit of study that deals with a good breakfast. The teacher says, "This is what a good breakfast should look like for all youngsters who want to grow up and be strong and fruitful Americans." The teacher shows her class a beautiful picture: It shows ham and eggs and a glass of milk and some toast. Pablo has just finished eating *chorizo con huevo* and tortillas at home. This little boy sees that his language is not used, and he sees that his breakfast is not what it should be.

The teacher also has a lesson on how a family should look. She goes to the files and picks a poster of how an American family should look. The poster shows a gentleman getting out of a car carrying a briefcase, a wife standing on the sidewalk waiting for him, two children, a boy and a girl, a dog named Spot, all in front of a brick home. Pablo thinks about this family and he says, "That's not how my family looks. I have a dirt floor at home. There's ten of us. We don't have a car. And our dogs all have a purpose on the farm." Not intentionally, because first-grade teachers do not operate this way, but clearly, she has communicated that Pablo's language is not important, the food he eats is not important and, certainly, his family looks strange.

What educators need to say is, "If you bring the language of Spanish to us, we are going to use that as a positive. We can use that language at the outset for concept and skill development. But, having said that, what is required? Success in this system requires a bilingual teacher. Also, it is okay to show that a good breakfast is ham and eggs with toast and milk; but then educators must also say, "Other families eat this, this and this, and they are all good. If you eat something different you can also become a strong American." And, the same must be said about how some families look. We must take advantage and use in a positive way what our students bring to school.

As teachers and administrators, we need to be ready to meet parents in as many different places as possible if we want them to participate and share their expertise; and they do have a lot of expertise. My mother could not read or write. She is now 92 years old, and she has about three Ph.Ds in life. It is critical that practitioners believe that even though parents may not be formally educated, they are able to help. We need to be prepared. If educators expect all parents to come to a place called school then we are in trouble. Teachers and administrators need to go to churches, to homes, to parents' places of work.

While in Pasco, I found that a lot of my parents were working in an apple-packing shed. I went out to that packing shed, spoke with the business owner, and asked, "Could I have a few minutes with your workers during their break? A lot of your workers are my parents. I want to talk to them about what is happening at school and how we want them to help us." He said, "Yes." In McAllen, I often had breakfast with parents in their homes. I went to the housing project and provided workshops that were needed. I set up a homework center there.

How do we involve parents? What are the practical things that need to be done? If educators are to make parents full partners then they must be active in developing a district-wide plan. In Pasco we are developing a five-year plan. My question to the parents is, "What is it that you want your schools to look like?" We ask about curriculum and instruction, personnel, student services—all of the areas that are part of a well-functioning school district. In Pasco, we ask parents to tell us what they think we ought to work toward, what they want for their children, what they want their children to look like when they graduate. By asking these sorts of questions, parents understand that they are being asked to be full partners in the education of their children. To be serious about partnership, educators must provide the resources to make it possible. As part of the major restructuring I undertook in Pasco, every campus will have a full-time home/school staff member responsible for making sure that parents are not forgotten. Parental involvement needs to be formalized.

The Contract

This volume has presented ongoing discussion about homework. If the instructional process is being used effectively—and lots of teachers know what I am talking about—if there is guided practice and youngsters are prepared for independent practice, there ought not to be much difficulty in preparing homework. Homework is really an assessment activity. Yet, many educators are bent out of shape about whether parents can help or not. Let me discuss what we have done in Pasco and McAllen. I said to my parents, "I want you to sign a contract. I want you to do the following things. As a parent, I will insist that all homework assignments are done each night." We do not ask parents to help their children with homework, and there is a reason for that. We want them to make sure that homework is completed.

The contract says,

> I will discuss at dinnertime what my child has learned at school each day. I will remind my child of the necessity of discipline in the classroom—especially self-discipline. I will provide for my child a minimum of one hour, three times a week, of interrupted MTV, which will be devoted to an instructional activity. And I will encourage support and praise my child everyday.

The contract is signed by the parent, the teacher, the student, the principal and the superintendent. We ask parents to place this signed contract somewhere in the home where they can see it every day; for example, the refrigerator door. If my parents cannot read English, the contract is in Spanish. If the parent cannot help with algebra, there is a telephone help line with a professional there to help the child.

Educators want parents to help, but sometimes parents do not know how to help. Therefore, we ask them, "What it is that you feel you need to know so you can do a better job as parents and participate in the activities that are essential to success in school?" I meet with a group of parents approximately once a month. I meet with them simply to engage in a dialogue. I ask them, "What is on your mind? What is it that is happening to you? What do I need to know? What are some of the questions you have?"

When asked, "What are the things you need to be better parents?" they answered with 40 different things. So I followed up, "What do you think we ought to do with that now?" I suggested a conference so that more people could talk to us about these different concerns and come up with a plan of action. Key among parents' concerns were keeping children out of gangs, ways to help a child be successful, and discussing sex with children. Perhaps 40 different "courses" were offered based on the concerns voiced. We held a conference for migrant parents, because they, too, want to help. We need to provide the process, the environment where their help can happen. I met with a team that had been empowered to be leaders in the migrant program. We talked about the conference and we talked about what went wrong and what went right. The point is that educators need to talk to parents before programs are developed.

Training can be provided in small groups in specific areas through a program called "Systematic Training for Effective Parenting." This program is a series of workshops that last six to eight weeks with topics, such as, how to listen to a child, discipline that develops responsibility, family meetings, and so on.

Among many immigrant or minority groups, families may not have graduated a single family member from high school. The notion of graduation from high school is not yet something they see as real. (By way of example, in my family there are six of us. The first two did not graduate; the third one did; and, thank God, I was number four. Now all children in my family will graduate.) We are trying to graduate the first born from high school. And we tell our parents to encourage their children to graduate. We tell them to wake their children up everyday by saying, "Juanito or John, wake up because you need to go to school. Because as soon as you finish high school and go on to college . . ." After a while, the youngster will say, "As soon as I finish high school and go on to college, then I'm going to do something else."

In Pasco we also have the traditional individual conferences, but we have added somethings to that in addition to a report card. We know how many students are below the twenty-fifth percentile and we know who they are. I asked my principals and teachers to put names to those percentages. We meet with parents and tell them that their child is below the twenty-fifth percentile. Next year, they will get a personal letter from the principal informing them that their child is below the twenty-fifth percentile. The principal will have to explain why the child scored poorly and what is going to be done about the child's progress. The principal will be asked to involve the parent to improve the child's score.

Communication

If the population is linguistically diverse, then you must use that language. We have a radio talk show in Spanish. It is interview format and airs at 7 a.m. when parents are preparing breakfast. We provide a lot of information at that time. As discussed earlier, I have a superintendent's council to meet with parents on a monthly basis. Newsletters go out to parents and these are bilingual. At the present, in Pasco, we are trying to decide whether to build more schools or to implement year-round education. We have prepared a newsletter describing both concepts and detailing when and how the school board will make a decision. We asked parents to comment on how they feel about year-round education.

Educators need to ask parents for help. Many parents believe the educator knows everything. I sent home a letter saying, "I need your help. Would you please sit down and talk to your kids about profanity?" The response was great! For the first time a superintendent had asked for help. Previously, the parents had thought that the superintendent knew everything. My letter helped them realize that is not true. This communication—asking for help, recognizing the need to participate—allows for volunteering of all kinds and at all levels.

When I arrived in McAllen, I said all children can learn. At that time, many replied that not only was I wrong, but they had data to prove me wrong. And they were right. The majority of the children in McAllen were failing, especially minority children. By the time I left the school of approximately 400 youngsters (almost 100% of these families were on welfare assistance), the children were scoring above the 90% proficiency rate on the state examination. In McAllen, we involved 80% of the parents in the classrooms every day. I then asked, "What else and how many other schools do I need in order to show you, and in order for you to believe, that all children can learn."

Resources

The greater community—those who do not have children in school—often does not become involved in school issues. And, the only time we visit them is when we need to pass a bond issue. To involve the wider community, we began an adopt-a-school program. We brought businesses into our schools to help our students. In McAllen, in the 8 years since the program began, over 300 businesses, individuals and small groups of people have adopted a school, a school program, or an individual student. We started a similar program in Pasco. In the first year, in just 3 months, we had over 40 participants with Westinghouse as our largest member. I explained to Westinghouse how Pasco schools needed their scientists' help. The scientists are now coming into our classrooms, working with our math and science teachers. And, our students are going to their plant.

We know that a lot of our households do not have a quiet corner with a chair and a desk for homework. We have opened our schools in the evening so that not only will the children come in to do their homework, but parents, also, will come in. Parents are learning English. For younger children we provide a place, too, so the evening center is a family affair. (You ought to see our parents working on computers alongside their children! These are parents who have not finished high school and may not know how to speak English.)

Conclusion

If the educator really believes that all children will be able to learn, then the tools will be found to enable them to learn. In 1993, some teachers say, "Not only do these kids belong below the twenty-fifth percentile, they will always be there and they will die there." Other teachers say, when asked, "Why does my child not bring home homework?" "Because our Mexican kids will not complete it anyway, so why bother?" If teachers and administrators want to bring parents in to help their children learn, then educators must set their house in order first and show the love and care for children, first, and for the parents, second. If educators do this, they will have a successful program.

8

School-Parent Partnerships: A Guide

Judy Daher

How do we apply knowledge about the importance of family involvement? How do we make family involvement real in districts, schools and classrooms? Family involvement, for the purpose of this discussion, includes the support and participation of parents at home and at the school site. In order for family involvement to have a positive impact, these objectives must be linked to the improvement of student achievement and to the quality of the learning and working environment of our students and staff.

This chapter discusses systemic change. While we are aware of many isolated positive events in our schools and in particular classrooms, if we are really talking about changing the way we do business in the field of education, we need to talk about systemic change. This kind of change is maintained regardless of who the principal is at the school or who the teachers are in the individual classrooms. I know through experience that this kind of change can be developed and implemented. While it is not an overnight process—it takes three to five years—the change can take place.

For system-wide efforts to work, educators need to begin with planning. The old adage, "If we don't know where we're going, we never know if we get there," is certainly true. Teachers and administrators need to establish objectives for involvement with recognizable milestones. Educators must delineate methods for regular input from the community, as well means for providing and receiving feedback from all parties involved, in order to report progress in the efforts to accomplish stated objectives. Everything included in this chapter has either been tried successfully in my schools or in my work in districts throughout this country and Mexico.

Much of the information found in this chapter originated in a program called the Quality Education Project, QEP.[1] My district adopted QEP in 1986 during my second year as principal. The program was so successful for my staff and for the parents at my school that I requested and received a leave of absence from 1990–1992 while I worked implementing QEP programs throughout the United States and Mexico. I can report on so many promising practices throughout our country from my two years of QEP work. But, I also learned through QEP that unless there is a systemic program, isolated efforts will not work long-term.

Structural Issues: Systemic Change

The process I discuss involves three generic issues: structure, staff and parents/significant adults. I begin with structural issues (see Figure 8.1). This process may appear to be hierarchical in nature, but it need not be. Suggested changes can be carried out in a collaborative mode. The establishment of a mission statement for the district or, barring that, for the school is the critical first step.

I am very proud of my home district, Redwood City, located in the San Francisco Bay Area. We are in dire financial straits, but rich in ideas and human resources. Our mission statement, shown in Figure 8.2, was established in 1983. From it, it is clear that the Redwood City School District will work in partnership with parents and the community to help youth develop a positive vision of the future. That mission statement is posted in every office in our district and in every school. It provides an unmuddled message to everyone that partnership is important for our district. The mission statement sets the tone for our outlook and all our activities.

I. Stuctural Issues: Systemic Change

   A. Mission statement: District/school

   B. School site plan

   C. Site administrator goal

   D. Teacher/staff goals

FIGURE 8.1

Redwood City School District
Redwood City, California

Mission Statement

The Redwood City School District will work in partnership
with parents and the community to help youth develop a positive
vision of the future and acquire the attitudes, knowledge and
skills necessary to become successful, contributing
participants in a rapidly changing world.

1986

FIGURE 8.2

Once a mission statement is in place, a school site plan is next. If family involvement and partnership is in the mission statement, it needs to be included in a site plan. I recommend site plans not segregate family involvement as a separate entity. We want to infuse family involvement throughout the life of the school. Some examples: If you are at the middle or the high school level and working on school climate issues, the question needs to be posed in a planning group (which should include parents), "How do we include family involvement to improve our school climate?" Or, if you are at the elementary school level where one of the focus areas is language arts, the question might be posed as, "How can we include families in the program to reinforce the instruction of language arts at this school?"

Likewise, if a mission statement is in the school plan, a certain amount of accountability is required. Site administrators must, therefore, include family involvement in their professional goals for the year. These can be integrated with other goals, but they must be there and site administrators must be accountable to the superintendent for those goals.

A site administrator should also ask teachers and support staff to include some type of family involvement objectives in their goals for the year. At staff goal-setting conferences, the site administrator can ask for three goals; family involvement needs to be included as at least one of the stated goals. I include teachers and staff because front office staff can make or break family relationships in schools. It is extremely important that they be included in this overall structural effort.

```
I. Staff Issues

   A. Education—Why, Who, What?
      1. Value of parent involvement
      2. Knowledge of families
      3. Specific strategies

   B. Time Management/Energy
      1. Don't do more, do it differently
      2. Analyze traditional activities
         "Why are we doing this?"
         "What makes sense?"

   C. Money—The least of our problems
```

FIGURE 8.3

What happens when these "windows of opportunities," as I call them, are opened? What happens once family involvement is established as a priority? I have observed some significant structural changes. At my school we tried a process of grouping parents whose children were having similar learning difficulties in the classroom. Group conferences were held in one-hour blocks instead of individual 15- or 20-minute parent/teacher conferences where little time is devoted to any one family. During that hour, the teacher explained, modeled and coached parents into reinforcement activities to help their children with learning at home. In grouped conferences, teachers expend the same amount of time, but with much greater impact on the instruction of those children.

Other examples are:

- "Families" of teachers who keep students for two years, teach all siblings of these students, and have personalized parent meetings
- Summer school activities for all families that require attendance at parent workshops
- Back-to-School Nights held on separate nights for each grade level to allow more time to discuss parents' role in the curriculum

These changes are basic and involve the way teachers do business; but they do not require contractual modifications and are relatively easy to implement.

In the Back-to-School Night example, the principal has to be out five or more nights, but the teachers only need to be out one night. This evening is altered from a one-way information process—"This is my discipline plan. These are the textbooks I use"—to an opportunity for parents and teachers to engage in a real dialogue about curriculum and what partnership means, specifically how parents can work with their children at home.

We Need You . . .

at our Annual Back-to-School Night.

Thursday, September 27
Kindergarten at 6:00 PM
Grades 1-3 at 6:30 PM
Grades 4-6 at 7:20 PM

You will have the opportunity to:

- *Meet with your child's teacher*
- *Find out about the programs and goals for this school year*
- *Get answers to questions you have about your child's school*
- *Enjoy visiting with other parents*
- *Find out how you can help your child succeed in school*

Questions about your child's progress will be dealt with at the Parent/Teacher Conference.

REMINDER: Student Pictures will be taken on Friday, September 28

FIGURE 8.4a

Back-to-School Night Evaluation

Dear Parents,

We want to make all of our school events useful and worthwhile to you! This year we tried a few changes, such as translators, no general session, Student Council guides, Info Expo, and child care for those who absolutely could not find sitters. We are interested in getting your honest opinion of these changes and your ideas about other improvements. We also want to know about what we're doing well. Please complete this form and return it to the Evaluation Boxes located in the main hallway. If you forget, send it to school office with your child tomorrow.

Why did you come to Back-to-School Night?

What was the best thing about Back-to-School Night?

What did you want that you didn't get?

Yes	No	No Opinion	
❏	❏	❏	Back-to-School Night was very useful to me.
❏	❏	❏	I received plenty of information in advance.
❏	❏	❏	The general presentation to all parents was informative.
❏	❏	❏	The classroom presentation by my child's teacher was helpful.
❏	❏	❏	Child care should be provided for those who cannot find sitters.
❏	❏	❏	Back-to-School Night was just the right length of time.
❏	❏	❏	The booths at Info Expo were imformative.

Suggestions for Improvement: What can we do better?

FIGURE 8.4b

The process must be confusing to parents. One teacher wants the parent to "monitor" the child's homework only. Parents must wonder, "What does that mean?" One teacher says, "I want you to sit next to your child and help." And another teacher says, "I want you not to help at all, but just to make sure the homework gets in." And these directions change from year to year, from teacher to teacher. Imagine the confusion for parents who have multiple children.

I think it is important for educators to question the purpose of Back-to-School Night. I believe that much of what schools actually do at Back-to-School Night can be accomplished in a written format. Why are we making people come to school to receive information they can read at home? Is it necessary for teachers to spend 10 minutes going through what happens at ten o'clock in the morning and what happens at one o'clock in the after-noon when that can be distributed in handouts? The real focus must be placed on implementing family involvement. What can we do with parents when they come to school to allow them to become part of the dialogue, to become partners with schools in the educational process?

Staff

In another successful implementation program, I offered kindergarten teachers an opportunity. I told them they would not have to work in first- and second-grade classrooms in the afternoon if they completed home visits. They all chose to do home visits. This was a very useful experience. It was extremely powerful for those teachers to see the homes of 102 kindergartners. (Only one family was not available for a home visit.) The visit directly affected the relationship of the teachers with those students and families. More important, those teachers talked about what they had seen during home visits in their conversations in the staff lunch room and at staff meetings. Many of the families of kindergartners had fourth-, fifth- and sixth-grade students. The home visit accomplished wonders for the knowledge base of our community. This kind of structural change can happen and it does not have to add costs to the budget.

Changing human behavior is difficult; it takes a long time for people to change. I think many problematic situations occur in schools because of our own—staff's own—doing. An anecdotal example: In my first principalship, I watched as the secretary registered new parents. These parents were predominately immigrants from Mexico. They were careful about the registration process. Inevitably, just on their way out, they asked, "What do we need to buy?" "What does my child need to bring to school?" "Do they need books?" "No," came the secretary's response. "We give them books." "Paper? Pencils?" "No, it's all taken care of." What do parents contribute, especially at the elementary school level? Nothing. And furthermore, we—the school—provide the child (my schools are Chapter 1) a free lunch and if the child can get here early enough, a free breakfast. And, while I believe we need to do these things in public education, the clear message parents leave with that first day is, "I don't have to do anything. This is wonderful. Everything is furnished for my child, even the basic necessities of food."

FIGURE 8.5

Teachers and administrators are in the "kid business," but in order to achieve our objectives of student academic success, we need to communicate well with adults. We often get what we expect: nothing. Staff must recognize the need for and utilize parent involvement; doing so requires creativity.

We now sit with parents and say, "You do not have to provide this, this and this. But, we have a folder that goes home every week with materials we expect you to review." The folder includes homework and work completed at school. We ask parents to initial homework and communicate by written note with the teacher if they have any questions. The folder has information about workshops we want them to attend. Information is provided about Back-to-School Night and other activities. Thus parents know that their responsibilities on some professional level may not be great, but their responsibilities for the education of their child are substantial. Staff will relate well to this kind of idea, acknowledging benefits if they change some of the ways they act.

The value of family involvement has been discussed extensively in this volume. For those practitioner-readers who still do not commit to it, I ask them at least to commit to trying it for a year.

Knowledge of families is very important, and I have made several references to two-way communication. We need to know more about our families, and if we are unable to do it through home visits we need to survey our parents. We can ask them, "What do you feel you need to do to help us develop a partnership role to focus on the success of your child?" Asking parents for their ideas makes things much less threatening. In new-teacher orientation sessions I devote time to the ways I work with parents. We have a school secretary in-service training every year in August. We devote 45 minutes to a discussion of public relations and ways of working with parents whose language is not one the secretary or teacher speaks. We discuss the cues and miscues we give them. We have mentor teachers in our district who help teachers, especially new teachers, in parent/teacher conferencing skills.

I have not been anywhere in the United States where a teacher preparation course provides hands-on experience to prospective teachers on how to conduct a parent/teacher conference effectively. In my own experience there were many times when a teacher came to me in tears during parent/teacher conferences. These teachers were terribly frustrated; they did not know how to work with a hostile parent, or a parent who is concerned about grades, or a parent who blamed the teacher for any lack of success on the part of the student. Now, we role play with our teachers, even during staff meetings, on how to work with difficult situations.

We use staff development days to talk about multicultural issues. For example, we know that in Mexico, division is taught in a format that is opposite to the process we teach. Imagine the confusion for children when they go home and ask for help. And we have already said to the parents, "Help your children." Many teachers who teach children from Mexican families are not aware of that difference. Simple things like that make a tremendous difference: Knowledge about all families and communication with them is essential to educating children well.

Five minutes of each staff meeting I hold is directed to family involvement. I may highlight a success and also a problem that a teacher had with parents. This emphasis establishes communication as a priority. How often do we ask our community what they need? And how often do we ask them how they feel about what we have given them? Do we ever ask parents before Back-to-School Night what skills or what information they need to help their children? Do we ever ask them afterward if they got the information they needed? We now hand out evaluation forms as they go into Back-to-School Night. We tell them, "Please fill this out. It's vital for us. We use it for planning for next year."

Time Management

As educators we are aware that staff feels overwhelmed. We know that staff is constantly approached with new programs and changes to the curriculum and instructional practices. But my advice is, *Don't do more, do it differently.* Educators must work smarter, work differently through analyzing our activities. We need to change our habits by asking ourselves, what makes sense? Educators must adapt to the 1990s when parents are no longer available during the day to call the school. Schools need homework hot lines because parents work every shift of the day and need help at varying times of the days. And schools need to restructure family involvement activities around these issues.

Communication

Communication needs to be practical, presented in a layperson's words, and in the native language whenever possible. Consistency in communication is critical, too. Educators need to present a consistent message.

When I was a principal I learned that if given an option, parents read a teacher's newsletter rather than a principal's. But, if asked to write a newsletter, teachers complain that this is the ultimate overload. They say they have no access to a computer and the newsletter must look good. Neither is necessary.

One of my own teachers developed a newsletter that is so manageable, I share it wherever I go. (This will not work well at the secondary level, but teachers can adapt it.) This teacher has a clipboard on her desk. Every time she wants to tell parents something, e.g., to practice multiplication tables, she writes the message on the clipboard. This process takes 15 seconds. When the page is filled and when it is the day of the week to send things

---

Communication

1. Make it practical

2. Layperson's language

3. Use the native language!

4. Be consistent in our communication

5. Present a consistent message

FIGURE 8.6

FIGURE 8.7

home, the "newsletter" is finished. The only "work" necessary is to duplicate the sheet. The newsletter has been written in no time at all and it is real communication. It is short, meaningful and very specific.

Consistent communication is also very important. In my district we use a QEP system that has been implemented throughout the country. All school communications go home in a folder on the same day every week. On the inside of the folder is a place for parents to initial that they have reviewed the enclosed materials, a place to write a note to the teacher, and a place for the teacher to respond. This procedure revolutionizes communication between home and school. It is consistent. Parents know what day school notices and corrected school work will come home. They have a couple of days to get it back to school. The folder helps organize families who may not be organized; and it also helps organize the school to have the folder ready to go home on the designated day. There is a bonus to this system. If representative work samples go

---

Progress Report

> **Hear Ye!**
> **Hear Ye!**

Name _____

Date _____

Outstanding = **O**   Satisfactory = **S**   Needs Improvement = **N**

Behavior
    Listened Quietly/Followed Directions   _____
    Did Not Disturb Others   _____
    Made Good Use of Time   _____
    Finished Work on Time   _____
    Got Along Well with Others (Indoors)   _____
    Got Along Well with Others (Outdoors)   _____

Academics
    Reading   _____
    Language   _____
    Spelling   _____
    Math   _____
    Homework   _____
    Effort   _____

Parent's Comments: _____
_____
_____

FIGURE 8.8

home, there are no surprises at parent/teacher conferences. There are no surprises because teachers have kept parents informed of how their children are doing.

Communication between school and family also includes the report card. My schools have changed from a quarterly reporting system to a trimester reporting system. In the last week of September or the first week of October, we have face-to-face parent/teacher conferences. These are not graded; that is, parents do not see the grades their children have attained. This is a "getting to know each other" conference. Teachers talk about the strengths of a child. And teachers ask parents, "What do I need to know?" It is a two-way communication: The teacher learns from the parent what she needs to know about a child as the year starts; and the parent learns what the teacher has seen from the child's performance during the early weeks of school. The conference is nonthreatening; it

---

Let's Talk!

Before the Parent Conference

Parent and child can discuss these questions before the parent/teacher conference.

1. What do you like about school?

2. What is your favorite subject?

3. What would you like to change about school? How would you change it?

4. Name one area that you would like to improve at school. What do you think you could do to improve it?

5. What is one good thing you would like me to tell your teacher about your year so far?

FIGURE 8.9

Before I Go

Thoughts Before the Parent/Teacher Conference

Take a few minutes to think through these questions before you go to the parent/teacher conference.

1. What do I believe my child does well at school and at home?

2. What concerns do I have about my child's progress?

3. Are there any specific problems or incidents that worry me?

4. What do I need to understand about the way the school or classroom operates?

5. Is there anything the teacher needs to know about my child in order for them both to have a successful year?

6. What is the main thing I would like to communicate to the teacher about my child?

FIGURE 8.10

Letter To My Child

Your teacher told me that she enjoyed you because . . .

Your teacher says that you were good at . . .

Your teacher says we might work at home on . . .

I promised that we would . . .

The thing I enjoyed most about your teacher was . . .

FIGURE 8.11

builds trust and sets the foundation for a relationship that will hold through the years. We are human beings and we will get into confrontational situations with other adults. But the way we deal with those confrontational situations is based on the trust built in good times.

Parent/teacher conferences can be made even more useful tools. At my schools three communications are sent home a couple of weeks before parent/teacher conferences: (1) questions as cues for parents who might not talk to their children about school, (2) an organizer for parents that asks them to think of one or two things they want to discuss with the teacher, and (3) some ideas to help parents talk to their children about what was discussed at the conference. The forms let parents know the conference is not a one-way communication, teacher to parents. These forms help legitimize the dialogue between parent and child, if it is not already there, and the dialogue between teacher and parent. At the conclusion of the conference we ask parents to write a note to their child; this lets the child know what the parents learned about the child at the conference. Or, the parent can talk to their child at home. In this way we show the child that the adults in his or her life care and work together with school for that child's academic success.

Figures 8.12 and 8.13 exhibit some of the things that can make the conference process much easier. Hanging a conference schedule outside the door helps parents know that they are at the right room. It also reminds them of their appointment time. Chairs and a table with educational reading material can be placed outside the conference room or classroom so that those parents who arrive early are comfortable, feel welcome and have something to do. A basket of toys for young children can be available while the parent is in conference. Sometimes these kinds of small things are extremely effective in making the environment more open.

Teacher _____

Room _____ Grade _____

(**Today's Conference Schedule**)

Time   Conference for . . .

FIGURE 8.12

**Please knock
on the door
when it is time
for your
appointment**
(Thanks)

FIGURE 8.13

The examples I have discussed point to communication as a critical element in the school's ability to educate. By asking parents what they think and feel about their children and the education process and about their concerns, the school conveys a basic message of shared responsibility. Responsibilities of school and parent are different but interdependent. By talking about these issues, parents get the message: Schools need parents!

We have a parent pledge, a student pledge, and a staff pledge. In some schools with high socioeconomic levels teachers have suggested

Elverta School District
Quality Education Project
Elverta Elementary Pledge

The Parent Pledge

I realize that my participation in my child's education will help his or her achievement and attitude. Therefore, I agree to carry out the following responsibilities to the best of my ability:

• see to it that my child attends school daily and arrives on time
• make sure my child gets approximately 8-10 hous of sleep each night and adequate nutrition
• encourage my child to complete his/her homework
• spend at least 15 minutes per day reading to/with my child (or equivalent of 75 minutes per week)
• review all school communications and return the weekly QEP folder/binder promptly
• attend Back-to-School Night, Parent-Teacher Conferences, Open House and other school events
• provide a quiet place for my child to study

_____   _____
Parent Signature   *Date*

The Student Pledge

I realize that my education is important. I know I am responsible for my own success. Therefore, I agree to carry out the following responsibilities to the best of my ability:

• arrive at school on time every day
• take my weekly QEP folder home to my parent(s)
• return completed homework on time
• be responsible for my own behavior
• be a cooperative learner
• ask for help when needed

_____   _____
Student Signature   *Date*

The Staff Pledge

We understand the importance of the school experience for every student and our roles as educators and models. Therefore, we will continue to carry out the following responsibilities to the best of our abilities:

• teach all the necessary concepts to your child for academic achievement
• strive to be aware of the individual needs of your child
• communicate with you regarding your child's progress
• provide a safe and healthy environment for your child
• correct and return assigned work in a timely way

_____   _____
Teacher   *Date*

_____   _____
Administrator   *Date*

© *Quality Education Project 1989*

White – Parent   *Pink – Student*   *Yellow – School*

FIGURE 8.14 *Source:* Quality Education Project

that the parents pledge not to overstress their children. This part of the pledge says, "I promise to balance my child's day with work, study and play." This legitimizes play for their children. The parent pledge—an articulated message—can be augmented by a subliminal one. School can send home a half-sheet of "thoughts" monthly to be placed on the refrigerator door. This reminder of good parenting techniques will be seen hundreds of times in a month.

Parent workshops are a crucial part of the family-school partnership. We send home a flyer that says what the workshop will address, what we hope to achieve, and that we need to take reservations so the school can provide childcare for the right number of children. The night prior to a workshop, parents call the people who have already said they will attend. We know that parents often do not keep personal calendars, and they sign up for an activity and then forget. With the call system we have 90% turnout rate for those who reserved. I have had 30-95 parents attend scheduled workshops. I have found that parents come when they feel the workshop is valuable and when they get something out of it. Workshops must be practical with hands-on activities. (If possible, create a video lending library of your workshops by videotaping them.)

It is my belief that the concern for funding is the least of educators' problems. It is important to know the resources that are available: Chapter 1, Title VII, SIP, EIA, private foundations and local businesses. It is the rare principal who cannot find $1000 if the cost is known in advance and the priority is there. (Folders, for example, which cost about $1.00 a child, are an excellent advertising vehicle for a local merchant.) The issues involved in school-family partnership do not really reflect funding, but attitude.

Parent/Significant Adult Issues

Families are so diverse. It does not make sense to ignore the role of the parent's significant other, or the adult relative living in the home, or even the high school student. Schools need to tap all family members, for they can play a valuable role with all students. In working with these adults, educators need to focus on the child by asking, "What's best for the child?" When the focus is on the child, ego needs diminish. For many parents who have not had pleasant school experiences, schools need to put a human face on what may appear to be a bureaucratic wall. The challenge is to change the human behavior of both staff and significant adults in our children's lives. In planning for greater involvement with families, ask what do parents or significant adults need to know to help their children be more successful and to provide a high quality

III. Parent/Significant Adult Issues

  A. What do parents need to know?

  B. How do they get the information?

  C. How do they know they're doing it right?

  D. Practical considerations that must be adddressed for widespread family involvement
    1. Time
    2. Child care
    3. Interest
    4. Transportation
    5. English language fluency
    6. Sense of not "belonging"

FIGURE 8.15

learning environment at home and at school? How do they get that information? And how do they know they are doing it right?

There are some practical considerations to keep in mind when planning for partnership. These are so logical that sometimes they are forgotten. *Time.* Survey your community for their best times. My Hispanic parents came out in force on Saturday mornings between 11 a.m. and 1 p.m. for parent workshops. That was not the best time for my Anglo community. Workshops for these parents were held during the evenings. (Beware soccer and Little League practice times!) *Childcare.* This is an absolute must for economic reasons. *Interest.* Parents will not come to school if they are not interested in a workshop topic. The topic needs to focus on what will improve education and success for their child and what will make their lives easier. *Transportation.* I once rented a bus for the first workshop at school. When we bring parents to school we offer them the opportunity to network. At the workshops, we tell the whole group that we have a lot of parents who do not have transportation but the parking lot has cars in it. I tell parents to figure out who lives close to one another. I ask them to pool their resources because buses are expensive. I have found this a successful way of handling the transportation issue. By renting a bus for the first workshop, educators give the gift of empowerment to parents: They can network with people in their own neighborhood for transportation purposes. *English language fluency.* Simultaneous translation does not work: Half of your audience is always bored, and they think this is the way bilingual education works. Nonprofit organizations in the community are funded for specific ethnic or language groups. These organizations provide workshops for immigrants or non-English speakers. The resources are available; schools need to establish linkages with these resources. *Belonging.* This is an issue for parent leaders because they are the school's ambassadors. Parents cannot be allowed to sit alone and feel isolated at school events. This builds anxiety. An anxious parent is unlikely to come back to school because he or she has no sense of belonging. Schools need to tap parents to approach these isolated parents.

Isolation is an important issue for parents who may not speak English or who—for a variety of reasons—may be uncomfortable in the school setting. To overcome these issues, start early. I suggest kindergarten orientation take place in June so that parents can be involved all summer. At orientation, distribute a basic bag of school supplies including the alphabet. Middle and high school orientation can also be held in June. A summer reading list can be distributed to parents. Educators must let families know they need to be involved. This process begins at the first school-family contact and continues all year. New parent orientation after the start of the school year will require individualized attention. One person in the school office can be designated to invest 30 minutes of time with the new family to discuss the school's system of family involvement. My experience proves this to be a worthwhile investment of time. If the new family is non-English speaking, appoint a foreign language ambassador to show this family "the ropes."

Vision and Change

Vision without Action > Dream

Action without Vision > Just Passes the Time

Vision with Action > **SUCCESSFUL CHANGE**

FIGURE 8.16

In conclusion, I want to address vision and action. Vision is wonderful, but without action, it is a dream. Action, without vision, without a plan, just passes the time, and takes a lot of energy. It is vision with action that brings successful change. The challenge is to coalesce educators' vision with actions, many suggested here, to promote successful change for all students.

Note

1. The Milken Family Foundation was one of the first major sources of funding for QEP beginning in the mid 1980s. Today QEP works with over 500,000 students throughout the United States.

PART FIVE

Forum for Exchange

9

Schools, Families and Communities: A Conversation with America's Educators

Cheryl L. Fagnano

The prominent role played by the teachers and principals who comprise the Milken National Educator Award Recipients is one of the distinguishing features of the program's annual conference. The conference is structured to elicit their ideas, opinions and experiences regarding important educational issues of the day. *Family, School and Community Involvement* was the topic they addressed at the 1993 National Educator Conference. Few connections are more central to working educators' success than the relationship between families and schools. Indeed, for nearly a quarter of a century, research on family involvement has shown that students have significant advantages when their parents support and encourage school activities (Clausen, 1966; Coleman et al., 1966; Mayeske, 1973; Heyns, 1978; Epstein and McPartland, 1979; Epstein, 1983). While this topic has singular importance for teachers' and principals' work lives, these professionals do not speak with a single voice, and often their opinions and ideas are shaped by their professional circumstances.

This chapter is a synthesis of over 50 hours of the Award Recipients' presentations of their own best practices as well as their discussions regarding family-school relationships. Assembled according to the demographic characteristics (socioeconomic status, ethnicity, and location or population density) of the student populations with whom they work, a total of 26 groups convened. Recounting their own experiences working with students and their families, the Award Recipients provided a rich and insightful narrative of family-school relationships from the practitioner's point of view. Occasionally, the practitioner's view diverged from the researcher's although much of the discussion reflected and verified the findings of both the social scientists present at the conference and others working in the area of family-school interactions.

Social Capital: The Practitioner's Point of View

James Coleman identifies parental involvement in children's schooling as a manifestation of social capital at work within a family. In research in this field, family background is highly correlated with student's performance in school. However, the variable of family background may not have been well-understood and consequently not well-measured in much of this research. Coleman (1987) asserts that the research examining the effects of various factors on student achievement considers "family background" as a single entity—and this is incorrect. Coleman contends that there are at least three distinct components to family background: financial capital, human capital and social capital. Financial capital is approximately measured by the family's wealth or income. It provides such resources as a place to do homework, books, newspapers or a home computer—resources that promote learning as well as financial resources capable of tempering family problems. Human capital is approximately measured by parents' education, skills and knowledge and provides the potential for an environment that will promote children's learning. Social capital is different from either of these. Social capital within the family provides children access to the adults' human capital and depends both on the physical presence of adults in the family and the attention given by these adults to the child. Social capital has to do with the *quality* of the relationship between people.

Additionally, the community and the schools are sources of social capital relevant to a child's development. And it is the presence of "social capital" within some families, schools and communities that Coleman speculates is responsible for the achievement gains of the students in those families, schools or communities. Moreover, Coleman asserts that access to a high level of social capital may promote children's school achievement irrespective of other socio-economic factors.

The term social capital may have been unfamiliar to many of the teachers and administrators who make up the Milken Educator Award Recipients. Still, the existence and the effect of social capital in the lives of their students is well-known to them. Regardless of the demographic characteristics of their students, the most frequently repeated sentiment expressed by the educators was a concern that parents interact with and support their children. This concern is summarized by the comments of several teachers when they said,

I don't need parents to come in and do reading or math with their child. I need them to make their child feel good about themselves, communicate confidently, and to love learning.[1]

What's important is the support, the caring, the love, the quality time that parents give children.

The sense of togetherness in a family is what makes the difference in many children's lives and school work.

Not only do the Milken Award Recipients know how important family and community relationships are to students, they actively encourage and support these relationships. Teachers at all grade levels reported assigning work to children that specifically would involve parents, grandparents, or even neighbors as active participants. Homework assignments and school activities intended to promote family interaction around children's education were common to most Award Recipients. Many teachers encouraged family conferences rather than the traditional parent-teacher only conference. One teacher developed a program intended to increase communication between parents and their children by allowing children to give their parents a report card.

Strengthening the link between home and school is a fundamental building block of school success. Milken educators do this in a variety of innovative and modern ways as well as relying on more traditional methods. In urban, rural and suburban school districts all over the United States, Milken teachers and principals are making old-fashioned home visits. They are getting to know the parents and families of the children they work with, because, as one teacher put it, "You can't imagine how effective and helpful it is to be able to say to a student: I know your mother and father, and I know they would want. . . ." However, home visits are not always possible, and even when possible they are often infrequent. Home-school communication on the other hand is best done on a regular basis. To this end, increasing numbers of teachers and principals are relying on modern technology. Most frequently, dedicated voice-mail systems allow teachers to leave information for parents of the entire class for an individual parent. In turn, parents are able to leave teachers messages during school hours, early in the morning or late at night, whenever their work schedules allow. Homework and attendance hot lines are in place so that parents can keep well-informed about their children's school life. Home videos of teacher conferences and back-to-school nights are commonly used to communicate with parents who are otherwise unable to attend.

Hungry, sick, or homeless children and children from dysfunctional families are not good candidates for school success. Parents of these children are often in need of assistance as much as the children. Milken educators know that schools cannot solve these pervasive social problems alone. To reverse the trend in declining social capital available to many children and families in our society, the entire community must become involved. As school is the *one* place where these children can be counted, Milken educators are in the vanguard of ongoing efforts to involve community members in schools and in bringing community services into schools. Some efforts are as ambitious as integrating full-scale social, medical and job-related services for students and their families into the schooling function. Some efforts involve simply inviting community members to visit the school, to adopt a classroom, or to provide funds to support needed programs and services. One educator organized local university students to work on a daily basis with bilingual children, while another organized parents and other community members to build a fence around the school to protect their children from the uncertainties and violence of urban life. One principal developed a school program for grandparents, aunts, uncles and community members who are not parents. This program is intended to develop extended family and community connections with the school, ultimately benefiting the students.

Regardless of the program or the activity, the goal is the same: to foster a solidarity between parents, community members and the school. Perhaps the most simple yet compelling declaration of how to involve the community in a school was made by an inner-city principal working very successfully with a community noted for its significant gang presence. "Just go out there and ask! That's all, just ask—and eventually you will be surprised at who helps and how much their help can mean."

Research on Family-School Relationships

The construct of social capital is a general one, useful in helping to understand the predicament of contemporary families and community life. It is clearly important for understanding family, school and community relationships and how they affect children's schooling. However, the work done on social capital does not represent the core educational research on family-school relationships. Illuminating this specific relationship is educational research in two areas. One branch of work focuses on the family and its characteristics, while the other branch focuses on the educational institution and its characteristics. Both seek to understand the various factors that influence family-school relationships and to make them stronger.

The family-focused research investigates such variables as social class, parents' education, language and family practice to explain the variation of parent involvement among families. This work suggests that there are distinguishing patterns of involvement linked to specific family characteristics. However, it is from the perspective of the school, the teacher and the administrator that the Milken educators are able to speak with the most authority.

The focal point of the Milken Award Recipients' discussions and presentations was the research on family-school connections, focusing on school culture and teachers' and administrators' practices and attitudes that can effect family involvement in education. This research investigates whether and how schools can successfully involve all parents in their children's education—especially parents who are not likely to become involved on their own (Epstein, 1990). Studies in this area frequently cite the unequal levels of parental involvement in the schools among parents from varying socioeconomic and ethnic groups and suggest that majority middle-class families often feel more welcome than working-class, poor or minority families do in many schools (Lightfoot, 1978).

In this light, the Milken educators raised their concerns regarding what they see as racism or classism within these schools. "What happens," they asked, "when teachers are racist, or when the kids and their families are racist?" It was noted that among teachers such negative attitudes often take the form of low expectations. One teacher commented, "Some teachers have this idea that black and Latino kids are going to drop-out, that they are not motivated and lack goals." Such attitudes lead not so much to aggressive negative behavior but to something much more pernicious: "a lack of trying, . . . lack of caring, . . . teachers giving up on a whole class of students." In response to this problem, most educators agreed with one teacher's statement, "The most important thing we can do as teachers is to rid ourselves of our own ghosts and stereotypes." But how?

Not surprisingly, the Award Recipients phrased the answer to this problem in educational terms. First, they recommended providing teachers and administrators who work in low-achieving schools (both minority and majority) with information about successful programs in use with similar populations. They concurred that a role model and an image of success are essential. Many teachers, it was suggested, have never seen a model of educational success of parental/school/community partnerships among poor, minority and non-English proficient students. Site visits to such places as the Vaughn Street School in Los Angeles were recommended. One participant noted, "Vaughn Street is a marvelous example of what can come from the cooperation and interaction between schools, families and community organizations. Teachers and administrators everywhere should visit it, talk with the principal and teachers and learn how to replicate it in ways that work for them."

Just as important as ridding one's self of negative stereotypes is working to eliminate them within the school and classroom. As one teacher said,

> It is the responsibility of the teacher in his or her classroom to not allow distrust and prejudice and to help children and their families work through it when it appears. Parent involvement plays a significant role in this effort. When parents and teacher know one another, when they understand one another and trust one another, when they work toward the same goals, the negative influences of racism and prejudice often can be mitigated.

Milken educators use a variety of methods to work through these types of problems. As much as the schools function as educational organizations, the institutions are also social organizations. As such, answers to difficult problems are often found in social events. Cultural awareness days, particularly those involving the sharing of food and fun, are frequently used to bring diverse people together. The recruitment of minority teachers and principals was seen as a partial solution to the problem of racism in the schools. Several Milken educators asserted that if more minority individuals held positions as teachers and administrators, minority children would be better served. Indeed, many of the educators identified teacher leadership, both minority and majority, as an essential component in making schools more welcoming to both minority and majority students and their families.

Teacher Leadership

Educational research verifies the anecdotal observation that teacher initiative can and does make a difference in parent-school relationships. Joyce Epstein's work has shown that some teachers are "leaders" in the effort to involve parents in their children's schooling. It has been noted that when parents are left on their own, the typical pattern continues to be greater involvement by better-educated parents and yields higher achievement by their children; less involvement by parents with lower levels of education yields lower achievement by their children (Baker and Stevenson, 1986; Entwisele, Alexander, Cadigan, and Pallas, 1986; Coleman, 1987). However, Epstein found in a study of single and working parents that when teachers reached out to parents who typically do not become involved with their children's schooling, they were generally more than willing to become involved. More impressive is Epstein's finding that, when teachers help parents to help their children, these parents can be as effective with their children as parents with more education, economic resources and leisure.

Milken Award Recipients are in the vanguard of American educators working to promote parent-school partnerships for all parents. At both the elementary and secondary levels, many are leaders in developing programs and activities that enhance and facilitate parent involvement in the education of their children. From breakfast orientation and information programs that accommodate working parents, to projects that bring parents into their children's history class as student participants, from parent recognition awards intended to create a welcoming climate in the school, to family journals and voice mail homework hot lines that keep parents informed about day-to-day school activities, these teachers and administrators are leading the way.

Yet, these same teachers expressed concerns about this leadership position. These educators voiced a concern that parents often see teachers as leaders, sources of support and resources in areas outside their field of expertise. Parents often call upon teachers to help them learn and develop basic parenting skills. Teachers repeatedly reported parents ask the question, "How can I deal with this problem?" Often the problem did not concern how the parent could help with homework or support their child's reading or math learning; the problem to which many parents referred concerned discipline issues, setting limits, dealing with children's emotional lives or staking out their own role as parents.

Furthermore, it is not uncommon for parents to seek guidance and help from teachers about a whole array of personal and family issues. The problems of homeless families; teenage mothers; families with drug, alcohol or sexual abuse problems; as well as neighborhood violence— are the problems teachers are confronted with as they attempt to involve families in their schools and classrooms. For many dislocated or single parents, the school is the primarily support institution for themselves and their families. But teachers legitimately worry that they are not prepared to teach parenting and other life skills, that they are not social or medical workers, and that often the funds are not available to hire appropriate counselors or social workers. Moreover, many suspect that when they take a leadership position, parents assume a subordinate position. They ask, "How do we take the position of someone teaching parents how to be parents and maintain the parents' feeling of equality in the parent-teacher partnership?"

Parent Involvement at the Secondary Level

The family-school relationship is influenced by many factors. Parents can be willing and able to take an active role and teachers may be prepared to be partners in the family-school relationship. Yet, there are times when little interaction is forthcoming. In fact, parent/family and teacher/school characteristics are not the only factors influencing family-school connections: The age and developmental needs of the student may play a role as well. There appears to be an inverse relationship between students' progression from level to level in school and parents' engagement in their children's schooling (Epstein, 1986; Stevenson and Baker, 1987). That is, more parents are actively involved in their elementary school-age children's education, while fewer are involved at the middle school level and fewer still at the high school level. Milken secondary teachers and administrators report that unlike elementary school parents, high school parents are difficult to find. The children themselves actually play a role in this absence. As one teacher noted, while a third-grader may just love to have mom come to school, an eleventh-grader would rather be shot at dawn. Adolescents may want to escape mom's apron strings, yet developmentally they are still in need of parent or parent-like involvement in their schooling. To meet these needs, programs that reach out to the wider community have been developed. Some schools have mentor programs using local industry volunteers who offer guidance and support for educational activities. Other schools have experimented with home visits or concentrated on involving parents in sports or social activities at school. Indeed, parental involvement appears to have a significant payoff in terms of student success regardless of the age of the student. Dornbush and Ritter (1988) reported that parent attendance at high school activities, such as athletic events or dramatic performances, is correlated significantly with children's school achievement, even when ethnic and social differences are controlled. In addition, they noted that just informing parents in a newsletter of the benefits accruing to their children by their involvement increased parental involvement.

Clearly parents want to help their children succeed in school, but often are uninformed regarding how they can help. Parents in large numbers report wanting the school to tell them how to help their children in school. These numbers remain high even for parents at the secondary level in both public and private schools (Epstein, 1986; Bauch, 1988; Dornbush and Ritter, 1988).

If parents want to be involved, and teachers want them to be involved, and moreover, if parent involvement leads to school success, it would appear there is little more to be said. However, an important issue remains: How do we define appropriate parent involvement?

Defining Parent Involvement

Few would disagree with the general proposition that parental involvement in children's education is both desirable and beneficial. However, among teachers and parents and even among different groups of teachers, the term parental involvement in education can have various and sometime contradictory definitions. Furthermore, the opinions of those in the school districts who make policy and allocate funds have a significant impact as well. In fact, depending upon the position and background of the individual there is often a wide discrepancy of opinion regarding what constitutes appropriate family or parental involvement in education or schooling.

For example, Carol Ascher, from the Institute for Urban and Minority Education at Columbia University, maintains that an important aim of educators today is to increase school effectiveness by improving the assistance they receive from parents (Ascher, 1988). In this effort Ascher maintains that schools must join with other community agencies to help. However, Ascher defines parent involvement in this context as parent's efforts to socialize their children at home in both informal and school-directed learning tasks. To meet Ascher's criteria of effective parent involvement, it is possible that a parent may never come to school or meet with a teacher. Socializing one's child to the norms of schooling and developing the attitudes, habits and disposition that promote school success is sufficient. Moreover, student achievement outcomes are not necessarily thought of as the only, or even the principal measure of, successful parent involvement. Development of citizenship and social values are judged to be of equal or greater importance to student academic achievement outcomes.

More traditionally, Williams and Stallworth (1983, 1984) reported in two studies that some principals and teachers favor only traditional parent-involvement activities, such as bake sales or attending class plays, but the majority of them do see more active forms of parent involvement, such as decision making, as useful or appropriate. This finding was supported by Menacker et al. (1988) who reported less than half (47 percent) of inner-city teachers surveyed believed in strong parental involvement, while only 30 percent believed that parents should "have a lot to say about how this school is run" (p. 109).

Epstein, on the other hand, identifies six types of parent involvement (see chapter 3 this volume) and suggests that for a fully effective parent involvement program, all six should be operating in a school. These include

(1) the basic obligations of families, including parenting skills and home conditions for learning at each age and grade level; (2) basic obligations of schools, including school-to-home and home-to-school communications about school programs and children's progress; (3) volunteers and audiences at the school or in other locations to support the school and students; (4) involvement of families in learning activities at home; (5) participation by families in decision making, governance and advocacy; and (6) collaborations with community groups and agencies to strengthen school programs, family practices and student learning and development.

The conference participants reported many "long discussions" among themselves and with the PTA representatives in their schools regarding the definition of parent involvement. Generally, it was agreed that there was no single definition of useful parent involvement. According to one educator, "It doesn't necessarily mean that parents just come to school, . . . often it's just an attitude at home, or perhaps asking questions from time to time about their children's schooling." While parent involvement is generally prized for its presumed effect on student achievement, many teachers hold that the true effect is an indirect one. That is, the true causal relationship is between student motivation and performance, and motivation is a by-product of the parents' interest and involvement in student learning.

However parent involvement is defined, whatever mechanism it works through to promote student achievement, the important point seems to be that it works. And because it works we are all obligated to foster productive parent/family-teacher/school relationships. As one teacher phrased it,

> Parents are our partners in the education of their children. We are professional teachers, they are professional parents. Each of us has a responsibility and just as it is not appropriate for the teacher to say, "Well, you should have learned that at home," parents should never expect that when they drop their child off at school that it now becomes our sole responsibility to educate the child. We are in this together.

Note

1. Award Recipient comments are excerpted from discussions at small group sessions held at the 1993 National Education Award Conference, March 24-26, 1993.

Bibliography

Allen, J., Barr, D., Cochran, M., Dean, C., and Green, J. (1989). "The Empowerment Process: The Underlying Model." *Networking Bulletin-Empowerment and Family Support*, I:1-12.

Anderson, J.D. (1988). *The Education of Blacks in the South, 1860–1935*. Chapel Hill, NC: University of North Carolina Press.

Ascher, C. (1988). "Improving the Home-School Connection for Poor and Minority Urban Students." *The Urban Review*, 20, 2:109-123.

Baker, D.P., and Stevenson, D.L. (1986). "Mother's Strategies for School Achievement: Managing the Transition to High School." *Sociology of Education, LIX*, 156-166.

Banks, J.A. (1993). "Multicultural Education: Historical Development, Dimensions, and Practice." *Review of Research in Education, XIX*, 3-50.

Bauch, P.A. (1988). "Is Parent Involvement Different in Private Schools?" *Educational Horizons, L*, 78-82.

Becker, G. (1964). *Human Capital*. New York: National Bureau of Economic Research, Columbia University Press.

Becker, H.J., and Epstein, J.L. (1982). "Parent Involvement: A Study of Teacher Practices." *The Elementary School Journal, LXXXIII*, 85-102.

Bell, D. (1973). *The Coming of Post-Industrial Society*. New York: Basic.

Caldwell, J. (1976). "Toward a Restatement of Demographic Transition Theory." *Population and Development*, 2, pp. 321-366.

Carnegie Corporation on Adolescent Development. (1993). *A Matter of Time: Risk and Opportunity in the Non-School Hours*. New York: Author.

Clark, R. (1983). *Family Life and School Achievement: Why Poor Black Children Suceed and Fail*. Chicago: University of Chicago Press.

Clausen, J.A. (1966). "Family Structure, Socialization and Personality." In L.W. Hoffman and M.L. Hoffman (Eds.), *Review of Child Development Research*, 2, pp. 1-53. New York: Russell Sage.

Coleman, J.S. (1987). "Families and Schools." *Educational Researcher, 16*, 32-38.

Coleman, J.S. (1990). *Foundations of Social Theory*. Cambridge, MA: Harvard University Press.

Coleman, J.S., et al. (1966). *Equality of Educational Opportunity*. Washington, DC: Government Printing Office.

Comer, J. (1980). *School Power: Implications of an Intervention Project*. New York: Free Press.

Conners, L.C., and Epstein, J.L. (1994). "Opportunities for Growth: School, Family, and Community Partnership in High Schools." Baltimore: Center on Families, Communities, Schools and Children's Learning.

Council on Families in America. (1993). *Eight Propositions on Familly and Child Well-Being.* (Available from The Institute for American Values, 1841 Broadway, Suite 211, NY, NY 10023).

Dauber, S.L. and Epstein, J.L. (1993). "Parents' Attitudes and Practices of Involvement in Inner-City Elementary and Middle Schools." In N. Chavkin (Ed.), *Families and Schools in a Pluralistic Society.* Albany: State University of New York Press.

Davies, D. (1988, April). "Hard to Reach Parents in Three Countries: Perspectives on how Schools Relate to Low-Status Families." Paper presented at the annual meeting of the American Educational Research Association, New Orleans.

Davies, D. (1990). "Shall We Wait for the Revolution? A Few Lessons from the Schools Reaching Out Project." *Equity and Choice,* 6(3), 68-73.

Delgado-Gaitan, C. (1990). *Literacy for Empowerment: The Role of Parents in Their Children's Education.* London: Falmer.

Delgado-Gaitan, C. (1991). "Involving Parents in the Schools: A Process of Empowerment." *American Journal of Education, C,* 1:20-46.

Delgado-Gaitan, C. (1992). "School Matters in the Mexican-American Home: Socializing Children to Education." *American Educational Research Journal, XXIX,* 3:495-513.

Demos, J. (1970). *A Little Commonwealth Family Life in Plymouth Colony.* Oxford: Oxford University Press.

Dornbusch, S.M., and Ritter, P.L. (1988). "Parents of High School Students: A Neglected Resource." *Educational Horizons, CXVI,* 75-77.

Entwisle, D.R., Alexander, K.A., Cadigan, D., and Pallas, A. (1986). "The Schooling Process in First Grade: Two Samples a Decade Apart." *American Educational Research Journal, XXIII,* 587-613.

Epstein, J.L. (1983). "Longitudinal Effects of Family School Person Interactions on Student Outcomes." In A. Kerckhoff (Ed.). *Research in Sociology of Education and Socialization* (4, pp. 19-128). Greenwich, CT: JAI.

Epstein, J.L. (1986). "Parents' Reactions to Teacher Practices of Parent Involvement." *The Elementary School Journal, LXXXVI,* 277-294.

Epstein, J.L. (1987a). "Toward a Theory of Family-School Connections: Teacher Practices and Parent Involvement." In K. Hurrelman, F. Kaufman, and F. Losel (Eds.) *Social Intervention: Potential and Constraints* (pp. 121-136). New York: DeGruyter.

Epstein, J.L. (1987b). "What Principals Should Know About Parent Involvement. *Principal, LXVI,* 6-9.

Epstein, J.L. (1987c). *Teacher's Manual: Teachers Involve Parents in Schoolwork (TIPS)* (Report P-61) Baltimore: Johns Hopkins University Center for Research on Elementary and Middle Schools.

Epstein, J.L. (1988). *Schools in the Center: School, Family, Peer, and Community Connections for More Effective Middle Grade Schools and Students.* Baltimore: Johns Hopkins University Center for Research on Elementary and Middle Schools.

Epstein, J.L. (1990) "Single Parents and the Schools: Effects of Marital Status on Parent and Teacher Interactions." In M. Halinan (Ed.). *Change in Societal Institutions* (pp. 91-121). New York: Plenum.

Epstein, J.L. (1991). "Effects on Student Achievement of Teachers' Practices of Parent Involvement." *Advances in Reading/Language Research: A Research Annual*, 5, pp. 261-276.

Epstein, J.L. (1992). "School and Family Partnerships." *Encyclopedia of Educational Research*, 6, 1139-1151.

Epstein, J. and Becker, H. (1982). "Teachers' Reported Practices of Parent Involvement: Problems and Possibilities," *Elementary School Journal, LXXXIII*, 2, pp. 103-114.

Epstein, J.L., and Conners, L.C., and Salinas, K.C. (1993). *High School and Family Partnerships: Surveys and Summaries.* Baltimore: Center on Families, Communities, Schools and Children's Learning.

Epstein, J.L., and Dauber, S.L. (1991). "School Programs and Teacher Practices of Parent Involvement in Inner-City Elementary and Middle Schools." *Elementary School Journal, IX*, 3:289-303.

Epstein, J.L. and Dauber, S. L. (1989). "Evaluation of Students' Knowledge and Attitudes in the Teachers Involve Parents in Schoolwork (TIPS) Social Studies and Art Program" (CREMS Report 41). Baltimore: Center for Research on Elementary and Middle Schools.

Epstein, J.L., and Herrick, S.C. (1991). *Implementing School and Family Partnerships in the Middle Grades: Three Evaluations of Summer Home Learning Packets, School Newsletters, and Orientation Days.* Baltimore: Johns Hopkins University Center for Research on Effective Schooling for Disadvantaged Students, CDS Report 20.

Epstein, J.L., Jackson, V., and Salinas, K.C. (1992). *Manual for Teachers: Teachers Involve Parents in Schoolwork (TIPS) Interactive Homework in Language Arts and Science/Health in the Middles Grades.* Baltimore: Center on Families, Communities, Schools and Children's Learning.

Epstein, J.L., and McPartland, J.M. (1979). "Authority Structures." In H. Walberg (Ed.). *Educational Environment and Effects* (pp. 293-310). Berkeley: McCutchan.

Flora, D. (1983). *State, Economy, and Society 1815–1975.* Vol. 1. Frankfurt: Campus Verlag.

Freire, P. (1970). *Pedagogy of the Oppressed.* New York: Continuum, 1970.

Gotts, E. (1980). "Long-Term Effects of Home-Oriented Pre-School Program." *Childhood Education, LVI*, 228-234.

Gutman, H. (1976). *The Black Family in Slavery and Freedom.* New York: Vintage Books.

Hamburg, D. (1992). *Today's Children.* New York: Times Books.

Heath, S.B. (1982). "What No Bedtime Story Means: Narrative Skills at Home and School," *Language in Society, XI*, 2, pp. 49-76.

Heath, S.B. (1983). *Ways with Words.* New York: Cambridge University Press.

Henderson, A. (1981). "Parent Participation—Student Achievement: The Evidence Grows." Columbia, MD: National Commission for Citizens in Education.

Herrick, S.C. and Epstein, J.L. (1991). "Implementing School and Family Partnerships in the Elementary Grades: Two Evaluations of Reading Activity Packets and School Newsletters." Baltimore: Johns Hopkins University Center on Research on the Effective Schooling of Disadvantaged Students, CDS Report 19.

Hess, R., and Shipman, V. (1965). "Early Experience and the Socialization of Cognitive Modes in Children." *Child Development, XXXVI,* 869-888.

Hewlett, S.A. (1991). *When the Bough Breaks: The Cost of Neglecting Our Children.* New York: Basic Books.

Heyns, B. (1978). *Summer Learning and the Effects of Schooling.* New York: Academic Press.

Hobbs, N. (1979). "Families, Schools, and Communities: An Ecosystem for Children. In H.J. Leichter (Ed.), *Families and Communities as Educators.* New York: Teachers College Press.

Jaynes, G.D., and Williams, R.M. (eds.) (1989). *A Common Destiny: Blacks and American Society.* Washington, DC: National Academy Press.

Jones, E. *et al.* (1986). *Teen-Age Pregnancy in Industrialized Countries.* New Haven, CT: Yale University Press.

Lareau, A. (1987). "Social Class and Family-School Relationships: The Importance of Cultural Capital." *Sociology of Education, LVI,* April, pp. 73-85.

Lareau, A. (1989a). "Family-School Relations: A View from the Classroom." *Educational Policy, III,* 3:245-259.

Lareau, A. (1989b). *Home Advantage: Social Class and Parental Intervention in Elementary Education.* New York: Falmer.

Lareau, A. (1993). "Family-School Relationships and Educational Policy: An Assessment." Paper prepared for Department of Education Conference, "Equity and Education: The Policy Uses of Sociology." Washington D.C.

Laslett, P. (1971). *The World We Have Lost.* London: Methuen.

Laslett, P. (ed.) (1972). *Household and Family in Past Time.* Cambridge, England: Cambridge University Press.

Leitch, M.L., and Tangri, S.S. (1988). "Barriers to Home-School Collaboration." *Educational Horizons, LXVI,* 70-74.

Lightfoot, S.L. (1978). *World's Apart: Relationships between Families and Schools.* New York: Basic Books.

Lorty, D. (1977). *School-Teacher: A Sociological Study.* Chicago: University of Chicago Press.

Martin, J.R. (1992). *The Schoolhome: Rethinking Schools for Changing Familes.* Cambridge, MA: Harvard University Press.

Mayeske, G., Okada, T., and Beaton, A. (1973). *A Study of the Attitude Toward the Life of Our Nation's Students.* Washington, DC: Government Printing Office.

McFate, K. (1991). *Poverty, Inequality and the Crisis of Social Policy: Summary of findings.*Washington, DC: Joint Center for Political and Economic Studies.

McPherson, G. (1972). *Small Town Teacher.* Cambridge: Harvard University Press.

Menacker, J., Hurwitz, E., and Weldon, W. (1988). "Parent-Teacher Cooperation in Schools Serving the Urban Poor." *Clearing House, 62,* 108-112.

Mitchell, B.R. (1962). *Abstract of British Historical Statistics.* Cambridge, England: Cambridge University Press.

Morrison, T. (1990). *Playing in the Dark: Whiteness and the Literary Imagination.* Cambridge, MA: Harvard University Press.

National Center for Education Statistics. (1992). *Digest of Education Statistics.* (United States Department of Education Publication NCES 92-097). Washington, DC: United States Government Printing Office.

Orgel, K. (1992). *A Report from the Chief Executive Officer.* (Available from The Decision Science Institute, 6301 W. 125 St., Overland Park, KS.)

Outtz, J.H. (1991). *The Demographics of American Families.* Washington, DC: Institute for Educational Leadership, Inc./Center for Demographic Policy and the Foundations of the Milken Families.

Parsons, T. (1959). "The School Class as a Social System: Some of its Functions in American Society." *Harvard Educational Review, XXIX,* 297-318.

Putnam, R.D. (1993). "Social Capital and Public Affairs." *The American Prospect, 13,* 35-42.

QEP (1993). *Program materials and implementation design.* (Available for QEP 690 Market Street Suite 1100, SF, CA 94104).

Rich, D. (1987). *Teachers and Parents: An Adult-to-Adult Approach.* Washington, DC: NEA.

Rich, D., Van Dien, J., and Mattox, B. (1979). "Families as Educators of Their Own Children." In R. Brandt (Ed.). *Partners: Parents and Schools* (pp. 26-40). Alexandria, VA: Association for Supervisors and Curriculum Development.

Schneider, B., and Coleman, J.S. (1993). *Parents, Their Children, and School.* Boulder, CO: Westview Press.

Scott-Jones, D. (1987a). "Families Influences on Cognitive Development and School Achievement." In E. Gordon (Ed.). *Review of Research in Education,* (pp. 259-304). Washington, DC: American Educational Research Association.

Scott-Jones, D. (1987b). "Mother-as-Teacher in the Families of High- and Low-Achieving Low-Income Black First-Graders." *Journal of Negro Education, XVI,* 21-34.

Scott-Jones, D. (1993). *Evaluating Education Reform: Parent and Community Involvement in Education.* Washington, DC: Government Printing Office.

Sigel, I.E., and Laosa, L.M. (Eds.). (1983). *Changing Families.* New York: Plenum Press.

Statistics Canada. (1976). *1921 Census of Canada: Occupations.*

Steinfels, P. (1992, December 27). "Seen, Heard, Even Worried About." *New York Times, Week in Review,* p. 3.

Stevenson, D., and Baker, D. (1987). "The Family-School Relation and the Child's School Performance. *Child Development, LVIII,* 1348-1357.

U.S. Bureau of the Census. (1975). *Historical Statistics of the United States: Colonial Times to 1970.* Washington, DC: Government Printing Office.

U.S. Bureau of the Census. (1992). *Statistical Abstract of the United States.* (112th ed.). Washington, DC: Government Printing Office.

United Nations. (1990). *1987 Statistical Yearbook.* New York.

Urquhart, M.C. and K.A.H. Buckley, (1965). *Historical Statistics of Canada.* Cambridge, England: Cambridge University Press.

Venezky, R., Kaestle, C., and Sum, A.M. (1987). *The Subtle Danger: Reflections on the Literacy Abilities of America's Young Adults.* Princeton, NJ: Educational Testing Service.

Waller, W. (1932). *The Sociology of Teaching.* New York: John Wiley.

Weber, M. (1947). *The Theory of Social and Economic Organization.* New York: Oxford University Press.

Williams, D.L., and Stallworth, J. (1983–1984). *Parent Involvement in Education.* Executive summary of final report, 1983–1984. Austin, TX: Southwest Educational Development Laboratory.

About the Editors
and Contributors

Editors

Cheryl L. Fagnano is vice president for educational programs and administration at the Milken Institute for Job & Capital Formation. She is responsible for the organization of the professional development program of the National Education Conference. Research interests have included teaching testing programs and faculty hiring practices. She received her doctorate in education from the University of California, Los Angeles.

Beverly Z. Werber joined the Milken Institute for Job & Capital Formation in the spring of 1993 as editor of the Institute's ongoing publications. She is a graduate of Harvard University in the field of Near Eastern Languages and Civilizations. Werber's previous publications for the Institute include *Educating a Twenty-First Century Public* and *The Challenge from Within.*

Contributors

James S. Coleman received his Ph.D. in sociology from Columbia University in 1955. He was an associate professor in the Department of Social Relations at The Johns Hopkins University and a former Guggenheim Fellow. Since 1973 Coleman has been a professor of sociology and education at the University of Chicago. Professor Coleman is the author of the landmark study *Equality of Educational Opportunity* (1966). His current research interests are in the social theory of norm formation and the functioning of schools. Coleman's publications include *The Adolescent Society* (1961), *Introduction to Mathematical Sociology* (1964), *The Asymmetric Society* (1982), *Public and Private High Schools: The Impact of Communities* (1987), *Foundations of Social Theory* (1990), *Equality and Achievement in Education* (1990), and *Social Theory for a Changing Society* (1991).

Judy Daher is director of magnet schools in the Redwood City Elementary School District in Redwood City, CA. She has a doctorate in education from the University of Southern California with an emphasis in policy planning and administration. As a bilingual/bicultural specialist in Hispanic parent-involvement strategies, Daher served as a consultant to educators in the state of Guanajuato, Mexico for the development of a plan for parent involvement. A long-time advocate for parent involvement, Daher has coordinated programs linking parents with the schools, including a federal bilingual demonstration project in Redwood City. Daher has taught and served in administrative capacities at the elementary, secondary and university levels for over 20 years.

Concha Delgado-Gaitan, associate professor of education at the University of California, Davis, received her Ph.D. in education and anthropology from Stanford University. Her paper "Early Childhood in Mexican American Families: From Tradition to Empowerment" was delivered at the Thematic Congress of Academic Scientific-Education in Intercultural Environments in 1991. A former elementary school principal, Delgado-Gaitan served as producer, director and editor of the Santa Barbara Television Studios video "Families and School: United for a Better Education." Author of *Literacy for Empowerment: The Role of Parents in Children's Education* (1990), she is also co-author of the book *Crossing Cultural Borders: Education for Immigrant Families in America* (1991), and editor of *School and Society: Learning Content Through Culture* (1988).

Joyce L. Epstein is co-director of the Center on Families, Communities, Schools and Children's Learning, principal research scientist, and professor of sociology at The Johns Hopkins University. She received her Ph.D. in sociology from Johns Hopkins in 1974. In 1991 Epstein received an Alvin C. Eurich Education Award in the area of family-school partnerships from the Academy for Educational Development. She has published extensively on the effects of schools, classrooms, family and peer environments on student learning and development. Her recent writings focus on middle grades organization, curriculum and instruction and their effects on early adolescents. She serves on the board of directors of the National Society for the Study of Education and the editorial boards of *Phi Delta Kappan, American Journal of Education, Review of Research in Education, The Urban Review* and *Education and Urban Society.*

Annette Lareau earned her Ph.D. in sociology from the University of California, Berkeley, and is an assistant professor of sociology at Temple University in Philadelphia. She is the author of *Home Advantage: Social Class and Parental Intervention in Elementary Education*, which won the American Sociological Association's Willard Waller Award for Distinguished Scholarship. Her current project, "Managing Childhood: Social Class and Race Differences in Parents' Management of Children's Organizational Lives," is an in-depth exploration of African American and

European American third-grade children. In this project, Lareau is comparing parental involvement in schooling, church, soccer, scouts, dance and other activities.

Lowell Milken is a co-founder of the Foundations of the Milken Families and has served as president since their inception in 1982. Mr. Milken formulated the Foundation's missions in the areas of education, community services, health care and medical research and human welfare. In addition to conceiving and implementing innovative programs with his brother Michael in all the Foundation's giving areas, he has been responsible for the expansion nationwide of a number of these programs. Mr. Milken has held positions of distinction in both the legal profession and the financial community. He graduated summa cum laude and Phi Beta Kappa from the University of California, Berkeley, and received his law degree from the University of California, Los Angeles Law School, having served as an editor on the *UCLA Law Review* and with distinction of the Order of the Coif.

Pablo Perez was the superintendent of School District No. 1 in Pasco, Washington where his educational focus has been parental involvement in childhood education. He is featured in the 1992 video "Involving Parents in Education," co-produced by the Association for Supervision and Curriculum Development and the McAllen Public School District, McAllen, Texas, where he served as superintendent of schools. After receiving his master's degree from Southern Methodist University in Dallas, Perez went on to East Texas State University in Commerce to earn his doctoral degree in education. Perez has served as both teacher and principal for the elementary schools in his hometown of Mission, Texas.

Diane Scott-Jones is an associate professor in the Department of Psychology at Temple University. Scott-Jones's interests are in social development and family processes of African Americans and other racial minorities. Her current research examines families' roles in their children's education and schooling and the educational and developmental outcomes of adolescent childbearers and their children. Professor Scott-Jones earned her Ph.D. in developmental psychology from the University of North Carolina, Chapel Hill. Her work has appeared in the *American Journal of Education, Journal of Adolescent Research, Phi Delta Kappan* and *Review of Research in Education*. She is a member of the editorial advisory boards of the journals *Early Education and Development, Educational Researcher, Review of Educational Research* and *Urban Education*.

Milken Family Foundation
National Educator Award
Recipients 1987–1992

Award Recipient	Position/School	State	Year
Carolyn Lott Adams	Principal & Attendance Ctr. Administrator *Oak Grove Schools*	Mississippi	1991
E. Norlene Adams	Teacher *Northside Elementary*	Nevada	1991
Katherine Afendoulis	Teacher *Meadow Brook*	Michigan	1991
Lea Albert	Principal *Kahuku High & Intermediate School*	Hawaii	1990
Eloise T. Alford	Teacher *Columbia Primary School*	Mississippi	1992
Margaret Allan	Teacher *Greenville Junior High School*	Illinois	1988
Janet S. Allen	Professor of Literary Eucation *University of Central Florida*	Maine	1991
Anne Alpert	Teacher *Columbus Magnet School*	Connecticut	1992
Jorge Alvarez	Teacher *Central High School*	Rhode Island	1991
Roberta Ameen	Teacher *National Mine School*	Michigan	1990
Willie Amos	Principal *Simmons High School*	Mississippi	1992
Deborah Anderson	Asst. Principal *Walter S. Christopher School*	Illinois	1989
Ronald Anderson	Principal *Harrison Street School*	Illinois	1992

Milken Family Foundation National Educator Awards are announced in the fall; the Conference is held annually the following spring.

Award Recipient	Position/School	State	Year
Evie Andrews	Teacher *Tualatin Elementary School*	Oregon	1990
G. Asenath Andrews	Principal *Catherine Ferguson Academy*	Michigan	1992
Neil Anstead	Coordinator/Teacher *Grover Cleveland High School*	California	1987
John G. Armstrong	Teacher/Coach *St. Mary's High School*	West Virginia	1992
Delia Armstrong-Busby	Principal *Mitchell High School*	Colorado	1990
James Aseltine	Principal *Irving A. Robbins Middle School*	Connecticut	1989
Steven Asheim	Teacher *Heritage High School*	Colorado	1991
Ede Ashworth	Teacher *Brooke High School*	West Virginia	1990
Elizabeth Asteriadis	Instructor *Glenn Hare Center*	Nevada	1991
Milton Baca	Principal *Andrew Jackson Middle School*	New Mexico	1992
Gary Bacon	Teacher/Program Director *Los Altos High School*	California	1992
Alfred Balasco	Teacher *Smithfield High School*	Rhode Island	1990
Brenda Sivils Ball	Teacher *Pine Bluff High School*	Arkansas	1992
Shirley Barber	Principal *Mabel Hoggard Sixth Grade Center*	Nevada	1992
James Barlow	Teacher *Aloha High School*	Oregon	1990
Edward Barrett	Principal *Analy High School*	California	1991
Linda Bates-Transou	Principal *Manual High School*	Colorado	1989
Debra R. Battle	Principal *Ranson Elementary*	West Virginia	1992
Barrie Becker	Teacher *Dorothy Kirby Center*	California	1989
Patricia Bell	Teacher *Shepardson Elementary School*	Colorado	1989
Sharon Belshaw-Jones	Principal *Fremont Unified School Disrict*	California	1988

Award Recipient	Position/School	State	Year
Richard Dale Benz	Teacher *Wickliffe High School*	Ohio	1992
Deveria A. Berry	Teacher *Martin Luther King Jr. Elementary School*	Connecticut	1991
Felica Ann Bryan Bessent	Vice-Principal *Valley High School*	California	1991
Leslie Bettencourt	Teacher *Lincoln Jr./Sr. High School*	Rhode Island	1991
Ann A. Billings	Research *Bowdoin College*	Maine	1992
Ronnelle Blankenship	Teacher *Ganns Middle Valley Elementary*	Tennessee	1992
John Blaydes	Principal *J. H. McGaugh High School*	California	1988
Jill Board	Teacher *Oakridge Elementary School*	Oregon	1991
Jewell Boutte	Program Manager *San Francisco State University*	California	1988
Charles Bowen	Principal *Broadmoor Junior High School*	Illinois	1988
Paul Bowen	Teacher *Petersburg High School*	Alaska	1990
Sheila Bowens	Teacher *Hamel Elementary School*	Illinois	1990
Rosemarye Boykins	Teacher *J. K. Harper Elementary School*	Georgia	1991
Bernard Bradley	Science Specialist *Newberry Math and Science Academy*	Illinois	1991
William Branch	Teacher *Evanston Township High School*	Illinois	1990
John Breaugh	Principal *Marvin Beekman Center*	Michigan	1991
Kathleen Brendza	Administrator *The Center*	Colorado	1991
Ronald Bright	Teacher-Coordinator *Castle High School*	Hawaii	1990
Cynthia Ann Broad	Teacher Consultant *Emma Y. Lobbestael Elementary School*	Michigan	1990
Sharon Brock	Principal *Boynton Elementary School*	Georgia	1990
Deb A. Brown	Teacher *Lakewood Elementary*	West Virginia	1991

Award Recipient	Position/School	State	Year
Frank Brusa	Principal *Las Vegas High School*	Nevada	1991
James Bryn	Teacher *Sparks High School*	Nevada	1990
Linda Bunch	Teacher *Independence Valley Elementary School*	Nevada	1988
Peter H. Burchell	Principal *Matansuka-Susitna Alternative School*	Alaska	1992
Nancy L. Burkland	Principal *Lincoln Elementary*	North Dakota	1992
Jean Burkus	Teacher *Amity Regional Junior High School*	Connecticut	1989
Susan Burt	Librarian/Teacher *Marlinton Middle School*	West Virginia	1990
Janie Pressley Butts	Teacher *Flanders Elementary School*	Connecticut	1990
Sue Ellen Cain	Teacher *Carrollton Junior High School*	Georgia	1992
Betty Campbell	Principal *Boise-Eliot Elementary School*	Oregon	1991
David A. Capaldi	Teacher/Department Chair *Toll Gate High School*	Rhode Island	1992
Carolyn Black Carbage	Teacher *Germantown Middle School*	Tennessee	1992
Joyce Carey	Teacher *Benjamin Franklin School*	Illinois	1989
Ronald Carter	Teacher *East St. Louis High School*	Illinois	1991
Michael Cassity	Learning Center Coordinator *Feather River Community College*	California	1988
Francis Chamberlain	Director of Instruction *Napa County Office of Education*	California	1987
Yvonne Chan	Principal *Vaughn Next Century Learning Center*	California	1991
Phyllis Cheaney	Principal *Lincoln School*	Illinois	1989
Linda Childers	Principal *Thurman G. Smith Elementary School*	Arkansas	1992
Kathy Chinn Chock	Teacher *Lunalilo Elementary School*	Hawaii	1992
Tom Christie	Teacher *Deerfield Elementary School*	Kansas	1992

Award Recipient	Position/School	State	Year
Anita M. Clark	Teacher *Marshall High School*	Michigan	1992
Walter J. Clark	Principal *Blatchley Middle School*	Alaska	1991
Linda Clement	Teacher *Metlakatla High School*	Alaska	1992
Elizabeth Clemons	Teacher *Creekside Elementary School*	Illinois	1989
Dora Cline	Teacher *Dillingham High School*	Alaska	1990
Margaret Clinkscales	Teacher *High Horizons Magnet School*	Connecticut	1988
Carolyn M. Coe	Principal *Mt. Iliamna Preschool*	Alaska	1992
Lois Cohn	Educational Media Consultant *McGaugh School*	California	1991
Frances Coleman	Teacher *Ackerman High School and Weir Attendance Center*	Mississippi	1991
Louise Coleman	Superintendent *Taft School*	Illinois	1989
Jacquelyn S. Combs	Principal *Stafford Community Schools*	Kansas	1992
Caroline Comi	Teacher *Hoaff Elementary School*	Colorado	1992
Christine Comins	Teacher *Pueblo County High School*	Colorado	1989
Norman Dale Conard	Teacher *Uniontown High School*	Kansas	1992
Jeannette Condon	Principal *Fort Fairfield Elementary School*	Maine	1990
Steve Connolly	Teacher *Cloverdale High School*	California	1987
Marilyn J. Cook	Teacher *Zephyr Cove Elementary School*	Nevada	1992
Teresa Corpuz	Principal *Albany Middle School*	California	1987
Rose Cousar	Teacher *Screven County High School*	Georgia	1990
Robert Cross	Principal *Century High School*	Illinois	1989
Rosemary Culverwell	Principal *F.W. Reilly School*	Illinois	1991

Award Recipient	Position/School	State	Year
John Mac Curlee III	Principal *Pearl High School*	Mississippi	1992
Mary Curtiss	Teacher *Trumbull High School*	Connecticut	1990
Joan D'Agostino	Teacher *Mt. Desert Island High School*	Maine	1990
Janet Daijogo	Teacher *Marin Country Day Elementary School*	California	1990
Dan Daniel	Teacher *Parkersburg High School*	West Virginia	1991
Phyllis Darling	Social Studies Curriculum Specialist *Clark County School District*	Nevada	1991
Mary Lofton Davidson	Teacher *The Mississippi School for Mathematics and Science*	Mississippi	1992
Edward Davis	Principal *Weaver High School*	Connecticut	1990
Jeanne E. Dawson	Teacher *Edward S. Rodes Elementary School*	Rhode Island	1990
Teresa de Garcia	Teacher *University Hill Elementary School*	Colorado	1989
Jerry L. DeLuca	Teacher *Tucker County High School*	West Virginia	1992
Francey Dennis	Principal *Silver Lake Elementary School*	Nevada	1989
David Dierking	Principal *Will C. Wood Middle School*	California	1991
Larry Dorsey-Spitz	Teacher *Hellbeck Elementary School*	Colorado	1991
Richard DuFour	District Superintendent *District 125*	Illinois	1988
John Duncan	Principal *Elderberry Elementary School*	California	1989
Robert Dyer	Teacher *Sea Road School*	Maine	1990
Mary Lee Edwards	Teacher *Yates Center High School*	Kansas	1992
William V. Edwards	Principal *Cimarron-Memorial High School*	Nevada	1988
Bonnie Elliott	Teacher *Bend Senior High School*	Oregon	1992

Award Recipient	Position/School	State	Year
Stephen C. Ellwood IV	Teacher *St. Francis Elementary School*	Maine	1991
Jaime Escalante	Teacher *Hiram Johnson High School*	California	1988
Karin Falkenstein	Principal, Spec. Ed. Supv., and G&T Coord. *Ottawa Elementary School*	Michigan	1992
Francine C. Fernandez	Principal *Kailua Elementary*	Hawaii	1991
Gary D. Field	Principal *College Park Elementary*	Georgia	1992
Bruce Fisher	Teacher *Fortuna Elementary*	California	1991
Cheryl Fisher-Allen	Teacher *Gilbert Stewart School*	Rhode Island	1990
Anita Fisk	Asst. Principal *Pershing County Junior-Senior High School*	Nevada	1988
Donna M. Fitzgerald	Asst. Principal & Teacher *Illing Middle School*	Connecticut	1991
Delores Aaron Flagg	Teacher *Blanchette Middle School*	Michigan	1991
Thomas A. Fleming	Teacher *Washtenaw County Juvenile Detention Ctr.*	Michigan	1992
James Ford	Principal *Henry D. Sheldon High School*	Oregon	1990
Malinda Frazier	Teacher *Lovelock Elementary School*	Nevada	1990
Joe G. Fresquez	Principal *Hernandez Elementary School*	New Mexico	1992
Claire Furukawa	Teacher *Kalani High School*	Hawaii	1991
Janis T. Gabay	Teacher *Junipero Serra High School*	California	1990
Don Gabriel	Teacher *Brush High School*	Colorado	1991
Teresa Gallman	Teacher *Woodbine Elementary School*	Georgia	1990
Peggy Gant	Teacher *Sparks High School*	Nevada	1992
Elizabeth Garand	Teacher *Northwest Middle School*	Connecticut	1988

Award Recipient	Position/School	State	Year
Gaylon Garner	Teacher *Ralph H. Metcalfe Magnet School*	Illinois	1988
Norma Garnett	Teacher *Toll Gate High School*	Rhode Island	1990
Frank D. Gawle	Teacher *Enfield High School*	Connecticut	1990
Jancie Gehrman	Teacher *William H. Brown School*	Illinois	1990
John Genasci	Principal *Sparks Middle School*	Nevada	1988
John H. Gengler	Principal/Teacher *Richardton-Taylor High School*	North Dakota	1992
Mary H. Giard	Teacher *Abraham Lincoln School*	Maine	1992
Shirley Gillis	Teacher *Harbor School*	Connecticut	1989
Larry Ginoza	Teacher *Waiane High School*	Hawaii	1991
Eula Mae Glenn	Teacher *Pelham Middle School*	Michigan	1991
S. Irving Granderson	Teacher *Elmwood Jr. High School*	Arkansas	1992
Pamela Granucci	Principal *Lincoln School*	Connecticut	1989
Patricia Grimmer	Teacher *Carbondale High School*	Illinois	1989
Mario Guerrero	Teacher *Jackson Elementary School*	California	1991
Lynne Haeffele	Math & Science Supervisor *Bloomington High School*	Illinois	1988
Thomas Hall	Teacher *Colquitt High School*	Georgia	1990
Elaine Hampton	Teacher *Zia Middle School*	New Mexico	1992
Pat A. Hartland	Teacher/ Teacher Trainer *Mendenhall River Community School*	Alaska	1992
Walter Hartung	Teacher *Nederland High School*	Colorado	1992
Timothy Harvey	Principal *William E. Fanning Elementary School*	California	1990
LeRoy E. Hay	Acting Superintendent *East Lyme Public School*	Connecticut	1988

Award Recipient	Position/School	State	Year
Sandee Gilletti Hay	Director, Federal Programs *Evans Elementary School*	Colorado	1990
David S. Heckman	Teacher *Monmouth Academy*	Maine	1991
Dollie Helsel-Felicetti	Principal *Grant Elementary School*	Illinois	1990
Suzanne Henning	Teacher *Tanana School*	Alaska	1990
Margarita C. Hernandez	Principal *Burton Elementary School*	Michigan	1990
James Hieftje	Principal *Fremont Middle School*	Michigan	1990
Edward E. Hightower	Principal *Eunice Smith Elementary School*	Illinois	1988
Ruby S. Hiraishi	Deputy District Superintendent *Windward Oahu District*	Hawaii	1992
Peter Hodges	Principal *Alicia Reyes Elementary School*	California	1989
Beverly Ann Hoffmaster	Teacher *Berkeley Heights Elementary School*	West Virginia	1992
Herbert Holland	Teacher *Crenshaw High School*	California	1990
David A. Hollowell	Teacher *Greeneville High School*	Tennessee	1992
Fred Horlacher	Teacher *Reed High School*	Nevada	1989
Kathleen M. Horvath	Teacher *Diekman Elementary School*	Illinois	1992
Nancy Housand	Teacher *Wynnton Elementary School*	Georgia	1991
Edward Howland	Teacher *Shasta High School*	California	1991
Richard A. Hunsaker	Teacher *Belleville West High School*	Illinois	1990
John Hurley	Asst. District Superintendent *Harlem Consolidated Schools*	Illinois	1990
Amy Ish	Teacher *El Gabilan School*	California	1989
Anna B. Jackson	Teacher *Carbondale High School*	Illinois	1992
Edward M. Jacomo	Principal *Friends School*	Michigan	1991

Award Recipient	Position/School	State	Year
Patricia M. Jarvis	Teacher *Bernon Heights Elementary School*	Rhode Island	1992
Benjamin Jimenez	Teacher *Garfield High School*	California	1989
Mae C. Johnson	Principal *Monterey High School*	California	1987
Cherry J.M. Jones	Principal & Professor *Flanders Elementary School*	Connecticut	1991
Louise C. Jones	Principal *George Washington Carver Elementary School*	California	1990
Mark Jordan	Teacher & Administrator *Gompers Fine Arts Option School*	Illinois	1989
Paul R. Kaufman	Teacher *Hillsdale High School*	Ohio	1992
Edward C. Keller III	Teacher *Mountainview Elementary School*	West Virginia	1990
M. Marjorie Kellogg	Teacher *Marietta High School*	Georgia	1991
Florence Steele Kidd	Principal *Head Middle School*	Tennessee	1992
Delise E. Kirkeide	Teacher *Harvey High School*	North Dakota	1992
Michael Klippert	Teacher *River Ridge Middle School*	Illinois	1991
Jack Knuston	Teacher *Plateau Valley High School*	Colorado	1991
Thomas Koeningsberger	Teacher *Guilford High School*	Illinois	1988
Jacqueline Kookesh	Teacher *Angoon School*	Alaska	1991
Roberta Koss	Teacher *Redwood High School*	California	1990
Peter Krasa	Principal *La Mesa Elementary*	California	1991
George S. Krelis	Principal *Wheeling Park High School*	West Virginia	1992
Leonora T. Kunimoto	Teacher *Waiakea High School*	Hawaii	1991
Gladys Labas	Principal *Maloney High School*	Connecticut	1992
Sandra A. Lamb	Teacher *Bradford Elementary School*	Rhode Island	1992

Award Recipient	Position/School	State	Year
William Langley	Principal *St. Viator School*	Nevada	1990
Daniel Lawson	Region Administrator *LAUSD; Elementary-District A*	California	1991
Mary Laycock	Math Specialist *Nueva Center for Learning*	California	1989
Margaret Leeds	Assistant Principal *Beverly Hills High School*	California	1987
Judith Essex Leonard	Math Resource Specialist/ Teacher Trainer *Southern RI Regional Collaborative*	Rhode Island	1991
William LePore	Teacher *Crater High School*	Oregon	1991
Richard Lindgren	Professor, Central CT State University *Illing Junior High School*	Connecticut	1988
Craig Lindvahl	Music Director *Teutopilos Grade School*	Illinois	1989
Jerry Linkinoggor	Principal *Clay County High School*	West Virginia	1990
Irene W. Llewellyn	Teacher *Laurel Elementary*	Connecticut	1991
Simon Lopez	Adult Education Coordinator *Rockwood Elementary School*	California	1987
Robert Lowry	Principal *Raymond J. Fisher Junior High School*	California	1989
Charles Lutgen	Principal *Woodland Park Middle School*	Colorado	1990
Patricia Mack	Principal *Walker Middle School*	Oregon	1992
George R. Mansfield	Executive Director *Educational Services Center*	Colorado	1991
Patrick Mara	Teacher *South High School*	Colorado	1990
Julia F. Marchant	Principal *Gardner School & Washington School*	Colorado	1992
Patricia C. Marden	Teacher *Belleview Elementary School*	Colorado	1991
Marvin L. Martin	Teacher *Zuni High School*	New Mexico	1992
Chiyomi Masuda	Teacher *Albany Middle School*	California	1991

Award Recipient	Position/School	State	Year
Jeniane Gee Matt	Teacher *Christine Sipherd Elementary School*	California	1989
Joseph Mattos	Principal *James H. Bean Elementary School*	Maine	1990
Gene McCallum	Administrator *Middle Schools Unity*	California	1987
Kevin McCann	Principal *Jamieson Elementary School*	Illinois	1990
Franklin R. McElwain	Teacher *Limestone Junior/Senior High School*	Maine	1992
Clyde McGrady	Principal *Staley Middle School*	Georgia	1990
Rae Ellen McKee	Teacher *Slanesville Elementary School*	West Virginia	1991
Charolette Meade	Teacher *Monogah Middle School*	West Virginia	1991
Robert Mellette	Program Director *Betsy Ross Magnet School*	Connecticut	1988
Paul Mello	Teacher *Middletown High School*	Rhode Island	1990
Marjorie Miller	Teacher *Longfellow School*	Maine	1991
Nola Kay Miller	Teacher *Washington Avenue Elementary*	New Mexico	1992
Sandra Perry Miller	Teacher *Portland Middle School*	Tennessee	1992
Winnie Miller	Teacher *Lake Oswego Junior High*	Oregon	1991
Valerie Mills	Teacher *Ypsilanti High School*	Michigan	1990
Priscilla Minkoff	Teacher *Lake Elementary School - Mentor*	Ohio	1992
Yvonne Minor	Principal *Walter H. Dyett School*	Illinois	1990
Tamiko Jobe Miyagi	Teacher *Academy for Math and Science*	Nevada	1991
Jean Miyahara	Technology Learning Center Coordinator *Waipahu High School*	Hawaii	1990
Cynthia Montoya	Librarian *James Gibson Elementary School*	Nevada	1990

Award Recipient	Position/School	State	Year
Christine Lynn Moore	Teacher *Orchard Park Elementary School*	Ohio	1992
Cosetta Moore	Independent Consultant *LA Unified School District*	California	1989
Roger Moore	Principal *Lake City Elementary School*	Michigan	1991
Donald J. Moran	Principal *Grant Elementary School*	Illinois	1992
Sharon Morgan	Teacher *Los Lunas Elementary School*	New Mexico	1992
Roger Morrissette	Teacher *Sedgwick Middle School*	Connecticut	1989
Norma Mota-Altman	Teacher *Emery Park Elementary School*	California	1990
Larry Moye	Teacher *Soltdana High School*	Alaska	1990
Ralph Murakami	Deputy District Superintendent *Department of Education*	Hawaii	1990
Connie Murphree	Teacher *Olive Branch Middle School*	Mississippi	1991
Irene Murphy	Principal *Mason Elementary School*	West Virginia	1991
Linda Murray	Teacher *Hyde Park Career Academy*	Illinois	1988
Darrell Myers	Teacher *Zane Jr. High School*	California	1989
Richard B. Nabel	Principal *Naugatuck High School*	Connecticut	1991
Lorna Mae Nagata	Principal *Mulberry Elementary School*	California	1988
K.C. Nainan	Teacher *Stone Mountain High School*	Georgia	1992
Sharon Nakagawa	Principal *Waialua Elementary School*	Hawaii	1991
Sheryl Nakonechny	Teacher *Clinton Rosette Middle School*	Illinois	1992
Nena Nanfeldt	Principal *Nathan Hale School*	Connecticut	1988
William Nave	Teacher/ Coordinator *Regional Alternative Program*	Maine	1990
Karen Nemetz	Principal *Mission Avenue Open School*	California	1989

Award Recipient	Position/School	State	Year
Bert Neumaier	Teacher *Farmington Public Schools*	Connecticut	1991
Barbra Neureither	Teacher *Holt High School*	Michigan	1991
David Neves	Teacher *Scituate Jr./Sr. High School*	Rhode Island	1991
Ron Nicholson	Teacher *Alsea School*	Oregon	1992
Jeffrey Norris	Teacher/Dept. Chair *Sparks High School*	Nevada	1992
Robert Nunez	Teacher *Eisenhower Middle School*	Illinois	1991
Rebecca S. O'Dell	Teacher *Leivasy Elementary School*	West Virginia	1992
Joyce O'jibway-Jennings	Teacher *Harbor Summit School*	California	1992
Cynthia J. O'Shea	Principal *Narragansett School*	Maine	1992
Philip Ogata	Teacher *Boulder High School*	Colorado	1990
Pamela Ogle	Teacher & Consultant *Waverly East Intermediate School*	Michigan	1991
Mary Omberg	Teacher *Nyssa High School*	Oregon	1990
Katherine Donner Owens	Teacher *Pascagoula Junior High School*	Mississippi	1992
Steven Parker	Principal *Joaquin Miller Junior High School*	California	1990
Judith Pavlak	Teacher *Channing Memorial Elementary School*	Illinois	1990
Bernard Pearce	Teacher/Coach *Ouray Schools*	Colorado	1992
Arthur Peekel	Teacher *Rolling Meadows High School*	Illinois	1991
Steven Pellegrini	Teacher *Yerington High School*	Nevada	1990
Louise Pempek	Teacher *Putnam Public Schools*	Connecticut	1989
Philip Perez	Deputy Superintendent of Instr. Services *Riverside Unified School District*	California	1988

Award Recipient	Position/School	State	Year
Yoriko Perritt	Teacher *Carver Math/Science Magnet School*	Arkansas	1992
John F. Pingayak	Bilingual Coordinator *Chevak School*	Alaska	1992
Wayne Piercy	Director of Legislative Services *Long Beach Unified School District*	California	1990
Klaire Pirtle	Principal *Kingsbury Middle School*	Nevada	1988
Larry Plew	Superintendent & Principal *Trinity Union High School Disrict*	California	1990
Linda Poff	Teacher *Straley Elementary School*	West Virginia	1990
Rod Poole	Counselor *Sitka High School*	Alaska	1992
Kathryn Porterfield	Teacher *Lynch View School*	Oregon	1992
Diane Price-Stone	Teacher *Philomath Elementary School*	Oregon	1990
John Putnam	Teacher *Washington Irving Junior High School*	Colorado	1989
Nelson W. Quinby III	Principal *Joel Barlow High School*	Connecticut	1989
David Rainey	Principal *AR School for Math & Science*	Arkansas	1992
Virginia Rebar	Principal *Haddam-Killingworth Middle School*	Connecticut	1990
Daniel Record	Teacher *Portland High School*	Connecticut	1990
Arthur Reisman	Teacher *East Leyden High School*	Illinois	1989
Margaret Reynolds	Teacher *Park View School*	Illinois	1990
Irving Richardson	Teaching Principal; Lead Teacher *Mast Landing School*	Maine	1992
Gayle Richter	Teacher *Zion-Benton High School*	Illinois	1989
Thomas Ridgeway	Teacher *Georgia Academy for the Blind*	Georgia	1990
Donald Ring	Lecturer of Secondary School Methods *Trinity College*	Illinois	1991

Award Recipient	Position/School	State	Year
Lucia Rivera	Principal *Bradford Elementary School*	Colorado	1989
Doris Robertson	Director of Grant Development *Fulton County Schools*	Georgia	1990
Sandra Robinson	Interim Superintendent *Department of Education*	Michigan	1990
Stephen M. Rocketto	Teacher *E.T. Grasso Southeastern Regional Vocational Technical School*	Connecticut	1992
Ann M. Rodgers	Principal *Hahira Middle School*	Georgia	1992
Michael Rodriguez	Counselor *Lee High School*	Arkansas	1991
Jacqueline Rogers	Teacher *Collins High School*	Mississippi	1992
Pamela Rolfe	Teacher *Limestone Junior-Senior High School*	Maine	1990
Mary E. Romero	Principal *Colfax Elementary School*	Colorado	1992
Larry D. Romine	Teacher *Lamar Middle School*	Colorado	1991
Elaine Rosenfield	Teacher *Sinsheimer Elementary School*	California	1987
Shirly Rosenkranz	Teacher *Temple City High School*	California	1987
James Roth	Teacher *Riverwood Elementary School*	Illinois	1990
Barbra S. Rous	Project Director *Director of Individualized Arts Program*	Georgia	1991
Patricia Rowe	Teacher *Lovelock Elementary School*	Nevada	1989
Kenneth Roy	Curriculum Director *Glastonbury Public Schools*	Connecticut	1989
William Dan Russell	Administrator *Johnson City Board of Education*	Tennessee	1992
Ruthanne Rust	Teacher *Denali Elementary School*	Alaska	1991
Donna Saiki	Principal *Hilo High School*	Hawaii	1990
Kenneth Sakatani	Teacher *Bayside Middle School*	California	1992

Award Recipient	Position/School	State	Year
Jennifer Salls	Coordinator *Bullis Curriculum & Instruction Center*	Nevada	1989
Drexel Sammons	Teacher *Crescent Elementary School*	West Virginia	1991
Carol Samsel	Teacher *Smalley Elementary School*	Connecticut	1990
Richard Sander	Teacher *Ketchikan High School*	Alaska	1991
Julia Sanders	Teacher *Pulaski County Elementary School*	Georgia	1991
Rhonda Schier	Teacher *Ponderosa Elementary School*	Colorado	1989
Edward Schroeder	Teacher *Coolidge Junior High School*	Illinois	1988
Stewart Schultz	Teacher *GMI Engineering & Management Institute*	Michigan	1990
Charles Etta Scott	Asst. Principal *Waycross High School*	Georgia	1991
Rodolpho Serna	Asst. Superintendent *Chicago Public Schools*	Illinois	1989
Virgil Sestini	Teacher *The Meadows School*	Nevada	1989
Thomas J. Sferes	Teacher *Kennebunk High School*	Maine	1991
Sylvia Shaina	Teacher *Thomas Edison Elementary School*	Michigan	1990
Kathy Sheiko	Principal *Green Elementary School*	Michigan	1991
Elaine G. Sherman	Curr./Admin. Specialist *Clark County School District*	Nevada	1992
Michelle Sherrill-Mix	Teacher *Hinks Elementary School*	Michigan	1992
April F. Shigemoto	Core Teacher/Curr. Coord. *Kauai High & Intermediate School*	Hawaii	1992
Cheryl M. Shintani	Teacher *Koloa School*	Hawaii	1992
Doris Shipp	Teacher *Doris Reed Elementary School*	Nevada	1988
Milton Shishido	Principal *Waipahu High School*	Hawaii	1991
James Simmons	Principal *Nelson Wilks Elementary School*	Arkansas	1991

Award Recipient	Position/School	State	Year
Judi Sloan	Teacher *Niles West High School*	Illinois	1992
Duane L. Small	Curriculum Coordinator *Waterville Public Schools*	Maine	1992
Ina Kaplan Smernoff	Teacher *East Hartford Middle School*	Connecticut	1992
Blanche F. Smith	Teacher *Decatur Classical School*	Illinois	1991
Dawn Smith	Assistant Principal *Warm Springs Elementary*	Oregon	1992
Lynn Smith	Teacher *Northside High School*	Arkansas	1992
Paula Smith	Teacher *Washington Elementary School*	Arkansas	1991
Robert Smith	Principal *South Kingstown Junior High School*	Rhode Island	1990
Sanderson Smith	Teacher *Cate School*	California	1988
Allan G. Snell	Principal & Curriculum Director *Washington Street School*	Maine	1991
John Snyder	Teacher *Cimarron-Memorial High School*	Nevada	1992
Margo Sorenson	Teacher *Harbor Day School*	California	1991
Gary D. Soto	Principal *Southridge Middle School*	California	1992
Dwight Souers	Teacher *Wilamette High School*	Oregon	1990
Carol Sparks	Teacher *Foothill Middle School*	California	1987
Shirley Splittstoesser	Teacher *Wiley Elementary School*	Illinois	1990
Joan Steinberg	Teacher *Presidio Middle School*	California	1988
Randy Steinheimer	Teacher *J. H. Freeman Elementary School*	Illinois	1988
Vivian Stephens	Teacher *Clairemont Elementary School*	Georgia	1990
Joyce L. Stevos	Administrator *Providence School Department*	Rhode Island	1992
Sharon M. Stites	Teacher *Washington Elementary School*	North Dakota	1992

Award Recipient	Position/School	State	Year
Susan Stitham	Teacher *Lathrop High School*	Alaska	1991
Tom Stone	Teacher *Sheldon High School*	Oregon	1991
Floyd Sucher	Professor of Elementary Education *Brigham Young University*	Alaska	1990
Harriss E. Sullivan, Jr.	Principal *Evans High School*	Georgia	1991
Marie Sullivan	Teacher *Sabin Junior High School*	Colorado	1990
Thomas Sullivan	Teacher *Valley Regional High School*	Connecticut	1988
Bertha Sutton	Principal *Monte Sano Elementary School*	Georgia	1991
Judith Kiernan Sweeney	Teacher *Lincoln Junior/Senior High School*	Rhode Island	1992
Jeffery Swenerton	Principal *Carmel Del Mar School*	California	1987
Carol J. Swinney	Teacher *Hugoton High School*	Kansas	1992
Patricia Swinton	Teacher *Provine High School*	Mississippi	1991
Koki Tamashiro	Teacher *State Distance Learning Teacher*	Hawaii	1992
Wayne Tanaka	Principal *Clark High School*	Nevada	1989
Harold Taylor	Teacher *Lincoln Early & Middle Elementary School*	Michigan	1990
Jean Tello	Teacher *A. A. Stagg High School*	Illinois	1988
Philip Terrell	District Superintendent *Pass Christian Public School District*	Mississippi	1991
Herman L. Thomas	Asst. Superintendent *Arkadelphia Public Schools*	Arkansas	1991
Jane Thompson	Principal *Palisades School*	Illinois	1988
Lynn Thompson	Teacher *Peoria Development Center*	Illinois	1991
Daniel Tilson	Teacher *Eastwood Elementary School*	Oregon	1992

Award Recipient	Position/School	State	Year
Charmaine Tinker	Principal *Sherwood Regional Alternative Middle School*	Ohio	1992
William Tinkler	Principal *Roosevelt School*	Connecticut	1992
Yvonne Toma	Teacher *Kipapa Elementary School*	Hawaii	1990
Nancy Toupal	Teacher *East Street Elementary*	Colorado	1990
Judy Trumble	Teacher *Edison School*	Illinois	1991
Joan Turner	Teacher *Matt Kelly Sixth Grade Center*	Nevada	1990
Phyllis Turner	Teacher *Monroe Elementary School*	California	1990
Jose Valderas	Director of Compensatory Education Progams *Dolsen Center*	Michigan	1991
John Vallino	Teacher *DeSoto Elementary School*	Illinois	1991
Susan Van Zant	Principal *Morning Creek School*	California	1989
Maria Azucena Vigil	Teacher *Las Lumas Elementary School*	California	1992
David Vigilante	Consultant *Gompers Secondary School*	California	1988
Carol R. Virostek	Teacher *Berlin High School*	Connecticut	1991
Mark Wagner	Teacher *Beullah Public School*	North Dakota	1992
Patricia Walker	Teacher *Bloom Trail High School*	Illinois	1991
Robert Wallace	District Superintendent *Cumberland School Department*	Rhode Island	1991
Darlene Walsh	Teacher *Greenbush Elementary School*	Rhode Island	1991
Ralph T. Watanabe	Principal *Kipapa Elementary School*	Hawaii	1992
Sidney Weathermon	Teacher *Martin Park Elementary School*	Colorado	1990
Connie Welsh	Principal *Collins Intermediate School*	Kansas	1992

Award Recipient	Position/School	State	Year
Eric D. Wertheimer	Principal *South Kingstown High School*	Rhode Island	1992
Carol R. Wheeler	Principal *Buckley School*	Connecticut	1990
Marilyn Whirry	Teacher *Mira Costa High School*	California	1988
Jeffrey White	Teacher *Trickum Middle School*	Georgia	1991
Debra White-Hunt	Teacher *Detroit-Windsor Dance Academy*	Michigan	1990
Canary Jane Whitfield	Teacher *Metter Primary School*	Georgia	1992
Eliot B. Wiggington	Teacher *Rabun County High School*	Georgia	1990
Lore Wiggins	Teacher *Gateway High School*	Colorado	1989
Kim Bridger Wilbanks	Asst. Principal *Fox Meadow Elementary School*	Arkansas	1991
Jackie Wilcox	Teacher *Cannon Ball Elementary School*	North Dakota	1992
Shereene D. Wilkerson	Principal *Willis Jepson Middle School*	California	1992
Virgil Wilkins	Teacher *Hundred High School*	West Virginia	1990
Deborah Willard	Director *Glastonbury Board of Education*	Connecticut	1988
Gordon M. Williams	Teacher *Trumbull High School*	Connecticut	1991
Jean Williams	Foreign Language Coordinator *Carrollton City Elementary School*	Georgia	1990
Thomas Williams	Teacher *Fayetteville High School*	Arkansas	1991
Vee Wilson	Principal *Grant Bowler Elementary School*	Nevada	1991
Edward Wong	Teacher *Vicksburg High School*	Mississippi	1991
Wilton Wong	Teacher *Capuchino High School*	California	1990
Harriet L. Woodard	Teacher *Stone Mountain Junior High School*	Georgia	1991
Deanna Gael Woods	Teacher *Wilson High School*	Oregon	1991

Award Recipient	Position/School	State	Year
Chuck Woodward	Teacher *Gateway High School*	Colorado	1992
Sandra E. Worsham	Teacher *Baldwin High School*	Georgia	1992
Donna York	Teacher *Romig Junior High School*	Alaska	1991
Pamela R. Young	Principal *Snowhill Elementary*	Ohio	1992
Robert D. Younker	Teacher *Southfield High School*	Michigan	1992
Charles Zezulka	Teacher *Carl C. Cutler Middle School*	Connecticut	1992

Index

About the Book

Most Americans will agree that, among other things, a quality education begins with meaningful interaction between families and schools. Yet as the contributors to this volume point out, several aspects of contemporary American society undermine the critical relationship among schools, families and their communities, and these conditions contribute to the current crisis in American education. This book brings together educators, public officials and community activists who examine the erosion of these bedrock institutions, offering a diagnosis of and prescription for what ails American education.

Blending theoretical analysis with practical insight, the authors of *School, Family and Community Interaction* consider the factors that encourage or compromise the relationship between today's schools and families. Included in their discussions are such key issues as the fragmentation of the family, the role of the family in children's development, minority and Spanish-speaking families' perspectives on schooling, family/school partnerships and the implementation of family/school/community partnership programs.

This volume offers perspective and vision for anyone wishing to create conditions among families, schools and their communities conducive to the successful education of America's children. It is essential reading for education specialists, public officials and policymakers, educators and community advocates.